SHABBAT

SABBATH
FOR MESSIANIC BELIEVERS

MESSIANIC HELPER series

Moedim: The Appointed Times for Messianic Believers
Messianic Sabbath Helper
Shabbat: Sabbath for Messianic Believers
Messianic Kosher Helper
Kashrut: Kosher for Messianic Believers
Messianic Fall Holiday Helper
Messianic Winter Holiday Helper
Messianic Spring Holiday Helper
Messianic Torah Helper

SHABBAT

SABBATH
FOR MESSIANIC BELIEVERS

J.K. McKee

MESSIANIC APOLOGETICS
messianicapologetics.net

SHABBAT

SABBATH FOR MESSIANIC BELIEVERS

Cover imagery: Deglee Degi/Unsplash

Published by Messianic Apologetics, a division of Outreach Israel Ministries
P.O. Box 516
McKinney, Texas 75070
(407) 933-2002

www.outreachisrael.net
www.messianicapologetics.net

Abbreviation Chart and Special Terms

The following is a chart of abbreviations for reference works and special terms that are used in publications by Outreach Israel Ministries and Messianic Apologetics. Please familiarize yourself with them as the text may reference a Bible version, i.e., RSV for the Revised Standard Version, or a source such as *TWOT* for the *Theological Wordbook of the Old Testament*, solely by its abbreviation. Detailed listings of these sources are provided in the Bibliography.

Special terms that may be used have been provided in this chart:

ABD: *Anchor Bible Dictionary*
AMG: *Complete Word Study Dictionary: Old Testament, New Testament*
ANE: Ancient Near East(ern)
Apostolic Scriptures/Writings: the New Testament
Ara: Aramaic
ATS: ArtScroll Tanach (1996)
b. Babylonian Talmud (*Talmud Bavli*)
B.C.E.: Before Common Era or B.C.
BDAG: *A Greek-English Lexicon of the New Testament and Other Early Christian Literature* (Bauer, Danker, Arndt, Gingrich)
BDB: *Brown-Driver-Briggs Hebrew and English Lexicon*
BECNT: *Baker Exegetical Commentary on the New Testament*
BKCNT: *Bible Knowledge Commentary: New Testament*
C.E.: Common Era or A.D.
CEV: Contemporary English Version (1995)
CGEDNT: *Concise Greek-English Dictionary of New Testament Words* (Barclay M. Newman)
CHALOT: *Concise Hebrew and Aramaic Lexicon of the Old Testament*
CJB: Complete Jewish Bible (1998)
DRA: Douay-Rheims American Edition
DSS: Dead Sea Scrolls
ECB: *Eerdmans Commentary on the Bible*
EDB: *Eerdmans Dictionary of the Bible*
eisegesis: "reading meaning into," or interjecting a preconceived or foreign meaning into a Biblical text
EJ: *Encylopaedia Judaica*
ESV: English Standard Version (2001)
exegesis: "drawing meaning out of," or the process of trying to understand what a Biblical text means on its own
EXP: *Expositor's Bible Commentary*
Ger: German
GNT: Greek New Testament
Grk: Greek
halachah: lit. "the way to walk," how the Torah is lived out in an individual's life or faith community
HALOT: *Hebrew & Aramaic Lexicon of the Old Testament* (Koehler and Baumgartner)
HCSB: Holman Christian Standard Bible (2004)
Heb: Hebrew
HNV: Hebrew Names Version of the World English Bible
ICC: *International Critical Commentary*
IDB: *Interpreter's Dictionary of the Bible*
IDBSup: *Interpreter's Dictionary of the Bible Supplement*
ISBE: *International Standard Bible Encyclopedia*
IVPBBC: *IVP Bible Background Commentary (Old & New Testament)*
Jastrow: *Dictionary of the Targumim, Talmud Bavli, Talmud Yerushalmi, and Midrashic Literature* (Marcus Jastrow)
JBK: New Jerusalem Bible-Koren (2000)

JETS: *Journal of the Evangelical Theological Society*

KJV: King James Version

Lattimore: The New Testament by Richmond Lattimore (1996)

LITV: Literal Translation of the Holy Bible by Jay P. Green (1986)

LS: *A Greek-English Lexicon* (Liddell & Scott)

LXE: *Septuagint with Apocrypha* by Sir L.C.L. Brenton (1851)

LXX: Septuagint

m. Mishnah

MT: Masoretic Text

NASB: New American Standard Bible (1977)

NASU: New American Standard Update (1995)

NBCR: *New Bible Commentary: Revised*

NEB: New English Bible (1970)

Nelson: *Nelson's Expository Dictionary of Old Testament Words*

NETS: New English Translation of the Septuagint (2007)

NIB: *New Interpreter's Bible*

NIGTC: *New International Greek Testament Commentary*

NICNT: *New International Commentary on the New Testament*

NIDB: *New International Dictionary of the Bible*

NIV: New International Version (1984)

NJB: New Jerusalem Bible-Catholic (1985)

NJPS: Tanakh, A New Translation of the Holy Scriptures (1999)

NKJV: New King James Version (1982)

NRSV: New Revised Standard Version (1989)

NLT: New Living Translation (1996)

NT: New Testament

orthopraxy: lit. "the right action," how the Bible or one's theology is lived out in the world

OT: Old Testament

PME: Practical Messianic Edition (author's rendering from *Practical Messianic* commentary series)

PreachC: *The Preacher's Commentary*

REB: Revised English Bible (1989)

RSV: Revised Standard Version (1952)

t. Tosefta

Tanach (Tanakh): the Old Testament

Thayer: *Thayer's Greek-English Lexicon of the New Testament*

TDNT: *Theological Dictionary of the New Testament*

TEV: Today's English Version (1976)

TLV: Tree of Life Messianic Family Bible—New Covenant (2011)

TNIV: Today's New International Version (2005)

TNTC: *Tyndale New Testament Commentaries*

TOTC: *Tyndale Old Testament Commentaries*

TWOT: *Theological Wordbook of the Old Testament*

UBSHNT: United Bible Societies' 1991 Hebrew New Testament revised edition

v(s). verse(s)

Vine: *Vine's Complete Expository Dictionary of Old and New Testament Words*

Vul: Latin Vulgate

WBC: *Word Biblical Commentary*

Yid: Yiddish

YLT: Young's Literal Translation (1862/1898)

A Summarization of Jewish Shabbat Traditions

Margaret McKee Huey and J.K. McKee

That the Jewish people have widely and faithfully observed the seventh-day Sabbath or *Shabbat* (שַׁבָּת)[1] throughout their history is a testament to God's declaration in Exodus 31:16: "The Israelite people shall keep the sabbath, observing the sabbath throughout the ages as a covenant for all time[2]" (NJPS). The view of a Conservative Jewish figure like Samuel H. Dresner, in his book *The Sabbath*, presses how "It is one of the basic institutions of humanity—an idea with infinite potentiality, infinite power, infinite hope, perhaps, as some claim, the single most significant contribution of Judaism to world culture."[3] The need for people to rest and sanctify a day unto their Creator has resonated for Torah-faithful Jews to be certain, as well as many Christian Believers, over the centuries.

If there is any area where today's Messianic movement tends to absolutely excel, it is with integrating a wide selection of the mainline Jewish traditions and customs for observing the Sabbath. Regardless of their background before coming to Messiah faith, religious or secular, today's Messianic Jews tend to remember *Shabbat* with the common elements of lighting candles, breaking *challah*, drinking wine, and attending synagogue services with traditional liturgy and Torah readings. Non-Jewish Believers who have been led by the Lord into the Messianic movement, seeking to

---

[1] Pronounced as *Shabbos* in the Ashkenazic Jewish tradition.

[2] Heb. *l'dorotam b'rit olam* (לְדֹרֹתָם בְּרִית עוֹלָם).

[3] Samuel H. Dresner, *The Sabbath* (New York: The Burning Bush Press, 1970), 14.

embrace more of the Hebraic and Jewish Roots of their faith, have also taken a hold of *Shabbat*, the opportunity for rest it offers to the people of God, and many of the significant traditions that can make the Sabbath a very holy and sanctified time.

The Hebrew term ***Shabbat* (שַׁבָּת)** itself mainly involves the "**day of rest, sabbath**" (*CHALOT*).[4] There is debate, for sure, regarding how close this noun should be associated with the verb *shavat* (שָׁבַת), "**cease, desist, rest**," with *TWOT* broadly noting that "There is still some question as to whether the noun *shabbāt* is derived from the verb *shābat*, or whether *shabbāt* is primary, and the verb derived from it. In any case, it should be observed that the meaning of *shābat* is 'to rest' in the sense of repose only when the verb is used in a Sabbath context."[5] Whether the Sabbath, for example, was instituted as a Creation ordinance *or* as just a memorial of Creation (cf. Genesis 2:2-3; Exodus 20:11), is a theological debate, with multiple sides represented among both Jews and Christians. Yet, even with some difference of opinion, the relationship of the noun *Shabbat* and verb *shavat* still communicates, as indicated by the *JPS Guide to Jewish Traditions* by Ronald L. Eisenberg, that this is a "day of rest and refraining from work."[6] One indeed is to cease and desist from normal activities on the Sabbath day.[7]

Those who recognize the importance of *Shabbat*, and the admonition for the seventh-day ("Saturday" on the Western calendar)[8] to be sanctified, enter into a special time between

---

[4] William L. Holladay, ed., *A Concise Hebrew and Aramaic Lexicon of the Old Testament* (Leiden, the Netherlands: E.J. Brill, 1988), 360.

[5] Victor P. Hamilton, "שָׁבַת," in R. Laird Harris, Gleason L. Archer, Jr., and Bruce K. Waltke, eds., *Theological Wordbook of the Old Testament* (Chicago: Moody Press, 1980), 2:902; also Ludwig Koehler and Walter Baumgartner, eds., *The Hebrew & Aramaic Lexicon of the Old Testament*, 2 vols. (Leiden, the Netherlands: Brill, 2001), 1407.

[6] Ronald L. Eisenberg, *The JPS Guide to Jewish Traditions* (Philadelphia: Jewish Publication Society, 2004), 125.

[7] Encountered in the Greek Septuagint and Apostolic Scriptures is the term *sabbaton* (σάββατον), "the Hebrew *sabbath*, i.e. *Rest*, N.T.; also in pl. of the single day, heterocl. dat. pl. σάββασι [*sabbasi*] (as if from σάββας [*sabbas*])" (H.G. Liddell and R. Scott, *An Intermediate Greek-English Lexicon* [Oxford: Clarendon Press, 1994], 722).

[8] Here we cannot overlook how our widely secular Western calendar is affected by terms originating in Greco-Roman paganism, as the seventh-day or "Saturday" does originate from the Old English "*Sæterdæg*, Saturn's day" (*Webster's New*

themselves, among themselves, and most importantly the Creator God. Keeping the Sabbath holy, both as a means of obedience to God and recognizing what it has meant to the Jewish people throughout the ages, is most vital for all of us. Most people in today's Messianic community do not think of *Shabbat* rest as a time when they can just sleep all day long; they do recognize that there are edifying and Spirit-inspired traditions, many of which were observed during the time of Yeshua of Nazareth, which should be followed today. The value of these traditions is witnessed in how they bring consistency to one's weekly routine, and a sense of unity and community to those who keep them. If there is anything negative to be observed, the exact places where many of the mainline Jewish *Shabbat* traditions originate, do need to be documented—from their origins in Scripture, Second Temple Judaism, or in post-Second Temple Rabbinic literature.

Sabbath is the Fourth Commandment

The seventh-day Sabbath or *Shabbat* is quite unique, in that it is not just a weekly observance for the people of God; it is the Fourth of the Ten Commandments. As Exodus 20:8 declares, *zakor et-yom ha'Shabbat l'qad'sho* (זָכוֹר אֶת־יוֹם הַשַּׁבָּת לְקַדְּשׁוֹ), "Remember the day, *Shabbat*, to set it apart for God" (CJB). The Sabbath is observed from what we reckon as sundown on Friday evening to sundown on Saturday evening, per the statement appearing multiple times throughout Genesis 1, "And there was evening and there was morning, one day" (Genesis 1:5), with the new day beginning in the evening.

There are a number of key admonitions surrounding *Shabbat*, which appear in the Torah or Pentateuch, later elaborated upon in the Tanach, and certainly appealed to in various ways in the Jewish theological tradition:

- ***Shabbat* is a memorial of God's Creation:** "Thus the heavens and the earth were completed, and all their hosts. By the seventh day God completed His work which He had done, and He rested on the seventh day from all His work which He had done.

World Dictionary and Thesaurus, second edition [Cleveland: Wiley Publishing, Inc, 2002], 568).

Then God blessed the seventh day and sanctified it, because in it He rested from all His work which God had created and made" (Genesis 2:1-3).

- ***Shabbat* is to be a permanent sign between God and His people:** "But as for you, speak to the sons of Israel, saying, 'You shall surely observe My sabbaths; for *this* is a sign between Me and you throughout your generations, that you may know that I am the LORD who sanctifies you'" (Exodus 31:13).
- **God's people must expel the effort to actually observe *Shabbat*, in order for the day to be made holy:** "Observe the sabbath day to keep it holy, as the LORD your God commanded you" (Deuteronomy 5:12).
- ***Shabbat* is to be a time when the Exodus of Ancient Israel from Egyptian servitude is remembered:** "You shall remember that you were a slave in the land of Egypt, and the LORD your God brought you out of there by a mighty hand and by an outstretched arm; therefore the LORD your God commanded you to observe the sabbath day" (Deuteronomy 5:15).
- ***Shabbat* is to be a time when people cease from their labors, in particular any heavy manual labor:** "You shall work six days, but on the seventh day you shall rest; *even* during plowing time and harvest you shall rest" (Exodus 34:21).

Most frequently, one sees in the Torah how the institution, of the seventh-day Sabbath or *Shabbat*, is closely tied to God's Creation of the world or the Exodus. Keeping the Sabbath is certainly connected to recognizing the God of Israel as supreme over the cosmos and the affairs of humankind, and in celebrating His salvation acts in history. It is to be astutely witnessed that while the Torah considered idolatry against God to be among the most serious of offenses (Exodus 23:24; Deuteronomy 4:25), that in the estimation of Eisenberg, "the exilic and post-exilic prophets considered profanation of the Sabbath the most damaging religious violation" (Isaiah 58:13-14; Ezekiel 20:11-12).[9] ***Shabbat* is not at all to be something just casually dismissed.**

Biblical Sabbath Observance

Throughout the Torah and Tanach, some key things were observed by the Ancient Israelites, in order to sanctify the Sabbath. A special offering of two lambs, in addition to the daily burnt offering, were presented at the Tabernacle/Temple (Numbers 28:9-10; cf. 1 Chronicles 23:31; 2 Chronicles 8:12-13; 31:2-3). Twelve loaves of showbread were to be presented at the Tabernacle/Temple (Leviticus 24:5-9; 1 Chronicles 9:32; 2 Chronicles 2:4). The severity of the Sabbath is realized in how an Israelite gathering wood was actually stoned to death (Numbers 15:32-36). While a cessation from general labor was to be recognized on the Sabbath, this did not apparently apply to guard duty at the king's palace in Jerusalem (2 Kings 11:4-12). It may also be deduced that various forms of travel likely did take place on the Sabbath (2 Kings 4:23-24).

The Torah and Tanach do mention various **types of work prohibited,** some of it specific. This included field labor (Exodus 34:21),[10] the kindling of a fire (Exodus 35:2-3),[11] commerce and various types of lifting heavy objects (Jeremiah 17:22;[12] Nehemiah 10:31;[13] cf. Amos 8:5), various forms of travel outside of a specific area (Exodus 16:29-30),[14] and treading wine presses and loading animals (Nehemiah 13:15-18).[15]

---

[9] Eisenberg, 127.

[10] "You shall work six days, but on the seventh day you shall rest; *even* during plowing time and harvest you shall rest" (Exodus 34:21).

[11] "For six days work may be done, but on the seventh day you shall have a holy *day*, a sabbath of complete rest to the LORD; whoever does any work on it shall be put to death. You shall not kindle a fire in any of your dwellings on the sabbath day" (Exodus 35:2-3).

[12] "You shall not bring a load out of your houses on the sabbath day nor do any work, but keep the sabbath day holy, as I commanded your forefathers" (Jeremiah 17:22).

[13] "As for the peoples of the land who bring wares or any grain on the sabbath day to sell, we will not buy from them on the sabbath or a holy day; and we will forego *the crops* the seventh year and the exaction of every debt" (Nehemiah 10:31).

[14] "'See, the LORD has given you the sabbath; therefore He gives you bread for two days on the sixth day. Remain every man in his place; let no man go out of his

While canonical Holy Scripture mentions various forms of prohibited work and activity, literature germane to Second Temple Judaism and the time following, would elaborate significantly—with differences of opinion and application to also be witnessed for sure—regarding how *Shabbat* was to be properly kept. This is especially true as the locus for observing *Shabbat* became focused more around the home and local synagogue.

The Importance of the Sabbath in Second Temple Judaism, and Major Sabbath *Halachah*

While the Torah or Pentateuch itself does issue various Biblical stipulations for observing the Sabbath, along with various applications present in the remainder of the Tanach—attempting to make the Sabbath holy, and evaluating what could and could not be done on *Shabbat*—constituted a major part of emerging Jewish practice in the post-exilic era. That there would be some significant discussions and debates emerge, following the end of the Babylonian exile, is hardly surprising, given the fact that non-observance of the Sabbath was believed to be one of the major factors responsible for the exile. The assertion of *Jubilees* 2:29 is, "Make known and recount to the children of Israel the judgment of the day that they should keep the sabbath thereon and not forsake it in the error of their hearts. And (make known) that it is not permitted to do work thereon which is unlawful, (it being) unseemly to do their pleasure thereon."[16]

---

place on the seventh day.' So the people rested on the seventh day" (Exodus 16:29-30).

[15] "In those days I saw in Judah some who were treading wine presses on the sabbath, and bringing in sacks of grain and loading *them* on donkeys, as well as wine, grapes, figs and all kinds of loads, and they brought *them* into Jerusalem on the sabbath day. So I admonished *them* on the day they sold food. Also men of Tyre were living there *who* imported fish and all kinds of merchandise, and sold *them* to the sons of Judah on the sabbath, even in Jerusalem. Then I reprimanded the nobles of Judah and said to them, 'What is this evil thing you are doing, by profaning the sabbath day? Did not your fathers do the same, so that our God brought on us and on this city all this trouble? Yet you are adding to the wrath on Israel by profaning the sabbath" (Nehemiah 13:15-18).

[16] O.S. Wintermute, trans., "Jubilees," in James H. Charlesworth, ed., *The Old Testament Pseudepigrapha*, Vol 2 (New York: Doubleday, 1985), 58.

Those who returned to reestablish a presence in the Holy Land, and be faithful to God's commandments, understandably wanted to develop systems whereby Jews could be considered obedient to the Sabbath instruction. With populations both in the Land of Israel and in a widespread Diaspora, the focus of *Shabbat* would decisively be one's localized home and localized Jewish community. Unlike various appointed times, such as *Yom Kippur* or Passover, and their required sacrifices[17]—it was much easier for the home to become the central nexus for observance of *Shabbat*. As the *Dictionary of Judaism in the Biblical Period* describes, "in the rabbinic period, [the Sabbath] attained a special place as a weekly observance that in the absence of the cult [and sacrifices], could continue as a family holiday practiced in individual homes."[18]

A wide degree, of very strict Sabbath regulations, is witnessed in the materials of the Qumran community. Among some of their significant practices include things that many would consider to be legitimate derivations of Torah instructions, while other things would be considered (quite) excessive by other sectors of Second Temple Judaism:

> "About the Sabbath, how to keep it properly. A man may not work on the sixth day from the time that the solar orb is above the horizon by its diameter, because this is what is meant by the passage 'Observe the Sabbath day to keep it holy' (Deut. 5:12). On the Sabbath day, one may not speak any coarse or empty word. One is not to seek repayment of any loan from his fellow. One may not go to court about property or wealth. One may not discuss business or work to be done the next day. A man may not go about in the field to do his desired activity on the Sabbath. One may not travel outside his city more than a thousand cubits. A man may not eat anything on the Sabbath day except food already prepared. From whatever was lost in the field he may not eat, and he may not drink unless he was in the camp. If he was on a journey and went down to bathe, he

[17] Obviously, there are components of the yearly appointed times that can be observed in homes, but the transition of the appointed times into a home and synagogue affair, was only completed after the destruction of the Second Temple.

Consult the relevant volumes of Messianic Apologetics' *Messianic Helper* series, on the Spring, Fall, and Winter holidays.

[18] "Sabbath," in Jacob Neusner and William Scott Green, eds., *Dictionary of Judaism in the Biblical Period* (Peabody, MA: Hendrickson, 2002), 538.

> may drink where he stands, but he may not draw water into any vessel. One may not send a Gentile to do his business on the Sabbath day. A man may not put on filthy clothes or clothes kept in wool unless he washes it in water or if they scrub it with spice. A man may not voluntarily cross Sabbath borders on the Sabbath day. A man may walk behind an animal to graze it outside his city up to two thousand cubits. One may not raise his hand to hit it with a fist. If it is uncooperative, he should leave it inside. A man may not carry anything outside his house, nor should he carry anything in. If he is in a temporary shelter, he should not take anything out of it or bring anything in. No one should open a sealed vessel on the Sabbath. No one should carry medicine on his person, either going out or coming in, on the Sabbath. No one should pick up stone and dust in an inhabited place. No caregiver should carry a baby on the Sabbath, either going out or coming in. No one should provoke his servant, his maid, or his employee on the Sabbath. No one should help an animal give birth on the Sabbath; and if it falls into a well or a pit, he may not lift it out on the Sabbath. No one should rest in a place near to Gentiles on the Sabbath. No one should profane the Sabbath for wealth or spoil on the Sabbath. Any living human who falls into a body of water or a cistern shall not be helped out with a ladder, rope, or other instrument. No one should offer any sacrifice on the Sabbath except the Sabbath whole burnt offering, for so it is written, 'besides your Sabbaths' (Lev. 23:38)" (CD 10.14-11.18).[19]

Also rather strict in their own right, are the various rulings witnessed in *Jubilees* 50:6-13:

> "And beyond the commandment of the sabbaths I have written for you and all of the judgments of its law. Six days you will work, but the seventh day is the sabbath of the LORD your God. You shall not do any work in it, you, or your children, or your manservant or your maidservant, or any of your cattle or the stranger who is with you. And let the man who does anything on it die. Every man who will profane this day, who will lie with his wife, and whoever will discuss a matter that he will do on it so that he might make on it a journey for any buying or selling,

---

[19] Michael Wise, Martin Abegg, Jr., and Edward Cook, trans., *The Dead Sea Scrolls: A New Translation* (San Francisco: HarperCollins, 1996), pp 68-69.

> and whoever draws water on it, which was not prepared for him on the sixth day, and whoever lifts up anything that he will carry to take out of his tent or from his house, let him die. You shall not do any work upon the day of the sabbath except what you prepared for yourself on the sixth day to eat and to drink and to rest and to observe a sabbath from all work of that day and to bless the LORD your God who gave to you the day of festival and the holy day. And a day of the holy kingdom for all Israel is this day among their days always. For great is the honor which the LORD gave to Israel to eat and to drink and to be satisfied on this day of festival and to rest in it from all work of the occupations of the children of men except to offer incense and to bring gifts and sacrifices before the LORD for the days and the sabbaths. This work alone shall be done on the day of the sabbath in the sanctuary of the LORD your God so that they might atone for Israel (with) continual gift day by day for an acceptable memorial before the LORD. And so that he might accept them forever, day by day, just as he commanded you. And (as for) any man who does work on it, or who goes on a journey, or who plows a field either at home or any (other) place, or who kindles a fire, or who rides on any animal, or who travels in sea in a boat, and any man who slaughters or kills anything, or who slashes the throat of cattle or bird, or who snares any beast or bird or fish, or who fasts or makes war on the day of the sabbath, let the man who does any of these on the day of the sabbath die so that the children of Israel might keep the sabbath according to the commands of the sabbaths of the land just as it was written in the tablets which he placed in my hands so that I might write for you the law of each time and according to each division of its days."[20]

Various of the stipulations seen above, in both the DSS and Pseudepigrapha, do include interpretations that would be adhered to, even today, among Jews keeping *Shabbat*. At the same time, it is hardly surprising that many of these sorts of regulations have stirred the interest of Biblical scholars, given how there are conflicts between Yeshua of Nazareth and various Jewish leaders, recorded in the Gospels, over Sabbath application. As is noted by S. Westerholm and C.A. Evans in the *Dictionary of New Testament Background,*

---

[20] Wintermute, in *The Old Testament Pseudepigrapha*, Vol 2, 142.

"With laws whose scriptural background seemed clear, and with customs long and widely established, many Jews could be expected to comply. It can also be seen, however, that questions of proper observance were often a matter of interpretation. The various religious parties of Jesus' day not infrequently differed in their practice. And though each group doubtless pressed on the others the claims of its interpretation to represent the will of heaven, such claims in our period were terrestrially unenforceable."[21]

Disagreements that would be detectable between the Messiah, and various Jewish leaders of the Second Temple period, would often be over observances of Sabbath restrictions that would be less strict than those witnessed at Qumran, among others. In *Jubilees* 50:8, intercourse between a husband and wife is prohibited on the Sabbath; in the Talmud it is (later) encouraged that sexual relations take place on the evening opening the Sabbath, *Erev Shabbat* (b.*Bava Qama* 82a;[22] b.*Ketuvot* 62b[23]). The Sabbath distance listed in CD 10.20 is a thousand cubits, whereas two thousand cubits (around a thousand yards if a cubit is regarded as being 17.5-18.0 inches) is the more standard distance for a Sabbath day's journey (cf. Exodus 16:29; Acts 1:12) witnessed in Rabbinical literature (m.*Eruvim* 4:3;[24] 5:7;[25] b.*Eruvim* 51a[26]).

---

[21] S. Westerholm and C.A. Evans, "Sabbath," in Craig A. Evans and Stanley E. Porter, eds., *Dictionary of New Testament Background* (Downers Grove, IL: InterVarsity, 2000), 1032.

[22] "That is on account of the requirement that sexual relations take place on Friday night, as it is written, 'That brings forth its fruit in its season' (Psa. 1:3), and said R. Judah, and some say, R. Nahman, and some say, R. Kahana, and some say, R. Yohanan, 'This refers to one who has sexual relations on Fridays'" (b.*Bava Qama* 82a; *The Babylonian Talmud: A Translation and Commentary*. MS Windows XP. Peabody, MA: Hendrickson, 2005. CD-ROM).

[23] "Said R. Judah said Samuel, 'Once a week, on Friday night.' 'Who brings forth its fruit in its season' (Psa. 1:3) – said R. Judah, and some say R. Huna, and some say R. Nahman, 'This refers to one who has sexual relations every Friday night'" (b.*Ketuvot* 62b; Ibid.).

[24] "He who went forth [beyond the Sabbath line] on a permissible mission, but they said to him, 'The deed already has been done,' has two thousand cubits in every direction [in which to walk about]" (m.*Eruvim* 4:3; Jacob Neusner, trans., *The Mishnah: A New Translation* [New Haven and London: Yale University Press, 1988], 214).

[25] "He who was in the east and said to his son, 'Prepare an *erub* for me in the west,' in the west and said to his son, 'Prepare an *erub* for me in the east,' if the

While the attitude at Qumran in the DSS was apparently *not* one of helping others on *Shabbat* who needed intervention (CD 11.13, 16), this is not the overall Jewish attitude, which was very much favorable toward helping others in various levels of distress. A general approach, as witnessed in the Mishnah, details how the prohibitions of working on *Shabbat* can be overridden—ranging from the need to give someone medicine to clearing away a building that has fallen on a person:

"Further did R. Mattiah b. Harash say, 'Who who has a pain in his throat—they drop medicine into his mouth on the Sabbath, because it is a matter of doubt as to danger to life. And any matter of doubt as to danger to life overrides the prohibitions of the Sabbath.' He upon whom a building fell down—it is a matter of doubt whether or not he is there, it is a matter of doubt whether [if he is there], he is alive or dead, it is a matter of doubt whether [if he is there and alive] he is a gentile or an Israelite—they clear away the ruin from above him. [If] they found him alive, they remove the [remaining] ruins from above him. But if they found him dead, they leave him be [until after the Sabbath]" (m.*Yoma* 8:6; further discussion in b.*Yoma* 85a-b).[27]

While the standard *halachah* or orthopraxy of the Pharisees was to be lenient in terms of a life needing to be saved on *Shabbat*, of critical importance are the thirty-nine main prohibitions, widely taken from Exodus 35, in terms of the activities required for the construction of the Tabernacle and Ark of the Covenant. The main list frequently referenced comes from m.*Shabbat* 7:2:

---

distance between him and his house is two thousand cubits, and between him and his *erub* is more than this distance, he is permitted to go to his house and prohibited from going to his *erub*" (m.*Eruvim* 5:7; Ibid., pp 217-218).

[26] "[If he said], 'My place of residence for the Sabbath is at its root,' he may then go from the place at which he is standing to the root, for a distance of two thousand cubits, and from the location of its root up to his house, for two thousand cubits. So he turns out to have the right to go four thousand cubits after it gets dark: [With regard to the rule that if he specified a particular spot of four cubits, he acquires it as his Sabbath locus and may walk to that place and another two thousand cubits beyond it to his home (Slotki),] *said Raba, 'And that is the rule only if by running toward the root he can get there before it got dark and the Sabbath began'*" (b.*Eruvim* 51a; *The Babylonian Talmud: A Translation and Commentary*).

[27] Neusner, *Mishnah*, 278.

> "The generative acts of labor [prohibited on the Sabbath] are forty less one: (1) he who sews, (2) ploughs, (3) reaps, (4) binds sheaves, (5) threshes, (6) winnows, (7) selects [fit from unfit produce or crops], (8) grinds, (9) sifts, (10) kneads, (11) bakes; (12) he who shears wool, (13) washes it, (14) beats it, (15) dyes it; (16) spins, (17) weaves, (18) makes two loops, (19) weaves two threads, (20) separates two threads, (21) ties, (22) unties, (23) sews two stitches, (24) tears in order to sew two stitches; (25) he who traps a deer, (26) slaughters it, (27) flays it, (28) salts it, (29) cures its hide, (30) scrapes it, and (31) cuts it up; (32) he who writes two letters, (33) erases two letters in order to write two letters; (34) he who builds, (35) tears down; (36) he who puts out a fire, (37) kindles a fire; (38) he who hits with a hammer; (39) he who transports an object from one domain to another—lo, these are the forty generative acts of labor less one."[28]

Another list, reflecting prohibited activities from the broad Second Temple period, is seen in m.*Beitzah* 5:2:

> "For (1) any act for which [people] are liable on grounds of Sabbath rest, for (2) optional acts, or for (3) acts of religious duty, on the Sabbath, are they liable in regard to the festival day. And these are the acts for which people are liable by reason of Sabbath rest: (1) they do not climb a tree, (2) ride a beast, (3) swim in water, (4) clap hands, (5) slap the thigh, (6) or stamp the feet. And these are the acts [for which people are liable] by reason of optional acts: (1) they do not sit in judgment, (2) effect a betrothal, (3) carry out a rite of *halisah*, (4) or enter into levirate marriage. And these are the acts [for which people are liable] by virtue of acts of religious duty: (1) they do not declare objects to be sanctified, (2) make a vow of valuation, (3) declare something to be *herem*, (4) raise up heave offering or tithe. All these actions on the festival they have declared [to be culpable], all the more so [when they are done] on the Sabbath. The sole difference between the festival and the Sabbath is in the preparation of food alone."[29]

---

[28] Ibid., pp 187-188; further discussed in George Robinson, *Essential Judaism: A Complete Guide to Beliefs, Customs, and Rituals* (New York: Pocket Books, 2000), pp 81-84.

[29] Ibid., 298.

While the Rabbinic tradition includes various stipulations regarding what is, and what is not, prohibited on *Shabbat*—stipulations that many Bible readers may conclude go well beyond the intention of the Torah commandments—it is important to be aware of much of the logic behind the Jewish religious leaders who formulated these rulings. The religious leaders of Israel were granted God-given authority to make judgments regarding Torah application, Deuteronomy 17:11 stating, "You must follow the laws as they interpret them; you must not wander to the right or to the left from the verdict they declare" (Scharfstein).[30] While one can be free to wonder about some of the reasoning behind making certain *Shabbat* prohibitions—with debates in future Jewish history certainly positing a difference between ancient levels of technology, and more automated and industrialized levels—the intention of such prohibitions was indeed not to defame the Sabbath, but rather to sanctify it. The Rabbinic intention behind some of the main prohibitions (m.*Shabbat* 7:2; m.*Beitzah* 5:2) was to keep people away from unnecessary work, and to get their attention focused on God—and was indeed influenced by the past tragedies, at least partially caused by Sabbath violation. *The New Encyclopedia of Judaism* addresses some of the significant Rabbinical logic in formulating various *Shabbat* prohibitions:

> "In order to prevent anyone from unwittingly transgressing any of the prohibitions, or doing something not in harmony with the spirit of the day, the rabbis enacted further rulings. Examples of these, which serve as a 'fence around the law,' are: *gezerot* ('decrees'...), e.g., a tailor should not go out just before sunset with a needle on him, lest he forget about it until after the onset of the Sabbath and 'carry' it (*Shab* 1:3); MUKTSEH ('set apart'), i.e., certain things should not be touched even if they are not forbidden as such, since this might lead to a prohibited act; *nolad* ('born'), i.e., something that comes into existence during the Sabbath, such as a freshly laid egg, is not to be used;

---

[30] Sol Scharfstein, *The Five Books of Moses, an Easy-to-Read Translation* (Jersey City, NJ: KTAV Publishing House, 2005), 483.

The issue of considering the Pharisees as having a consultative authority for matters of Torah *halachah*, is discussed in the exegesis paper on Matthew 23:2-3, "Who Sits in the Seat of Moses?" by J.K. McKee, appearing in the *Messianic Torah Helper*.

> and *shevut*, i.e., an act not in the spirit of the day, for example climbing a tree (*Béts.* 5:2).
>
> "Rabbinical sources devote much space to discussing the prohibition against carrying objects. One is not to carry them from the public domain to the private and vice versa, and from one point to another within the public domain. Since this may involve effort under certain circumstances, and in order to allow carrying in the prohibited areas, they formulated the ERUV, involving legal devices making carrying possible within a determined area."[31]

Many of the discussions on what is, and what is not, proper for the Sabbath are witnessed in the Talmud tractate *Shabbat*. One will certainly find, as indicated by the *Dictionary of Judaism in the Biblical Period*, how "In rabbinic law, each category is subjected to further expansion through the delineation of derivative varieties of forbidden labor. In some interpretations, this yields as many as 1,521 forbidden activities (Y. Shabbat 7:1, 9b-c)."[32] An observation made in the Mishnah is, "The laws of the Sabbath, festal offerings, and sacrilege—lo, they are like mountains hanging by a string, for they have little Scripture for many laws" (m.*Chagigah* 1:8).[33] One can surely see how a figure like Yeshua of Nazareth could indeed observe, "Woe to you *Torah* experts too! You load people down with burdens they can hardly bear, and you won't lift a finger to help them!" (Luke 11:46, CJB). While there are useful, and perhaps even edifying, principles to be found in the Rabbinic tradition surrounding *Shabbat*—keeping track of all of these regulations, *often at the expense of the Torah commandments themselves*, can be an unnecessary burden.

In much, much later times, with the emergence of Reform Judaism, and subsequently Conservative Judaism, in the Nineteenth Century, significant adaptations of the Rabbinic stipulations surrounding *Shabbat* would be made. These would often have to account for a much different situation for modern Jews, not living

---

[31] "Sabbath," in Geoffrey Wigoder, ed. et. al., *The New Encyclopedia of Judaism* (Jerusalem: Jerusalem Publishing House, 2002), 667.

[32] "Sabbath," in *Dictionary of Judaism in the Biblical Period*, 539.

[33] Neusner, *Mishnah*, 330.

in the same Ancient Near Eastern or Mediterranean conditions in which these directions were originally formulated.[34]

One needs to have an as-balanced-as-possible approach when reviewing extra-Biblical instructions on Torah practices like *Shabbat*, especially in view of the Apostle Paul's word that his fellow Jewish people "were entrusted with the oracles of God" (Romans 3:2), with it needing to be recognized how *logos* (λόγος) has a wide variety of applications, including things that are "chiefly oral" (*BDAG*).[35] It is up to the people of God, filled with His Holy Spirit, to sift through some of the Rabbinic materials—widely claimed to be the Oral Torah or Oral Law—and discover "whatever is true, whatever is honorable, whatever is right, whatever is pure, whatever is lovely, whatever is of good repute" (Philippians 4:8).

Some of the principal Talmudic opinions surrounding *Shabbat* reveal how significant the Sabbath has been to the Jewish people throughout history. It is fair to say that these sentiments have some useful things to communicate, that others highlight how important Sabbath observance has been approached, and that some others go far beyond the intention of the institution:

- ***Shabbat* is a precious gift given by God to Israel:** "*So, too, it has been taught on Tannaite authority:* 'That you may know that I the Lord sanctify you' (Exo. 31:13): The Holy One, blessed be He, said to Moses, 'Moses, I have a fine gift [for you] in my treasury, and it is called Sabbath, and I desire to present it to [the people of] Israel. Go and inform them'" (b.*Shabbat* 10b).[36]
- **those who delight in *Shabbat* will be granted their heart's desire:** "Said R. Judah said Rab, 'To anyone who makes the Sabbath a time of rejoicing they give whatever his heart desires: "Delight

---

[34] Dresner, pp 80-81 includes a Conservative Jewish modern list of work for consideration; Mark Dov Shapiro, *Gates of Shabbat: A Guide for Observing Shabbat* (New York: Central Conference of American Rabbis, 1996), pp 49-59 includes a similar one for the Reform movement.

[35] Frederick William Danker, ed., et. al., *A Greek-English Lexicon of the New Testament and Other Early Christian Literature*, third edition (Chicago: University of Chicago Press, 2000), 599.

[36] *The Babylonian Talmud: A Translation and Commentary*.

yourself also in the Lord and he will give you your heart's desires" (Psa. 37:4). Now I don't know what this "delight" is, but when it says, "and you shall call the Sabbath a delight" (Isa. 58:13), you must say, that refers to the pleasure of the Sabbath'" (b.*Shabbat* 118b).[37]

- **observance of two successive Sabbaths is key to bringing about the final redemption:** "Said R. Yohanan in the name of R. Simeon b. Yohai, 'If the Israelites keep two successive Sabbaths in a proper manner, they will be saved immediately: "Thus says the Lord concerning the eunuches that keep my Sabbaths" (Isa. 56:4), followed by, "even them will I bring to my holy mountain" (Exo. 56:7)'" (b.*Shabbat* 118b).[38]
- **a special spice is to be used for Sabbath dishes, which is actually the Sabbath itself:** "Said Caesar to R. Joshua b. Hananiah, 'How come the food cooked for the Sabbath has such a wonderful fragrance?' He said to him, 'We have a special spice, called "Sabbath," which we put into it, and its fragrance is wonderful.' He said to him, 'Give us some.' He said to him, 'It works only for someone who keeps the Sabbath, but it doesn't work for someone who doesn't keep the Sabbath'" (b.*Shabbat* 119a).[39]
- **those who observe *Shabbat* are thought to be participants with God in His Creation:** "For said R. Hamnuna, 'Whoever says the Prayer on the eve of the Sabbath and says the Sabbath verses, "And the heaven and the earth were finished" (Gen. 2:1), is regarded by Scripture as though he had become a partner of the Holy One, blessed be He, in the works of creation, as it is said, "And the heaven and the earth were finished" (Gen. 2:1) — don't read the

---

[37] Ibid.

[38] Ibid.

[39] Ibid.

words to yield "finished" but rather "and they finished."' Said R. Eleazar, 'How on the basis of Scripture do we know that speech is equivalent to action? "By the word of the Lord were the heavens made" (Psa. 33:6)'" (b.*Shabbat* 119b).[40]

- **prayer before *Shabbat* is thought to purge one of sins:** "Said R. Joshua b. Levi, 'Whoever says the formula, "Amen, may his great name be blessed," with all his strength — they tear up for him the decree that has been issued against him: "When retribution was annulled in Israel, for the people offered themselves willingly, Bless you the Lord" (Jud. 5:2). Why was "retribution annulled"? Because "the people offered themselves willingly."' R. Hiyya bar Abba said R. Yohanan [said], 'Even if he is marked by a taint of idolatry, they forgive him. Here it is written, "when retribution was annulled," and elsewhere, "And Moses saw that the people had broken loose for Aaron had let them loose" [and the words for annulled and broken loose correspond] (Exo. 32:25)'" (b.*Shabbat* 119b).[41]
- **a Sabbath violator is considered to be the same as an idolater:** "...the apostate, of one who pours libations [before idolatry], and of one who violates the Sabbath in public" (b.*Chullin* 5a).[42]

While there are a diverse array of Talmudic opinions present surrounding *Shabbat*, that the Sabbath was taken seriously by many Jewish people during the time of Yeshua, and immediately after, cannot be avoided. Some of these sentiments were probably present during the Judaism of Yeshua's time, and would have been agreed with, in various parts, by the Messiah and His early followers. Others would clearly be disregarded. And then, some others would be toned down. As Paul observed in Romans 10:2, "For I testify about them that they have a zeal for God, but not in accordance with knowledge." Many religious Jews of the First

---

[40] Ibid.

[41] Ibid.

[42] Ibid.

Century period and onward were indeed quite serious about their belief in the God of Israel, but they did not always have the appropriate knowing of Him to go along with it.

A hugely significant feature of ancient *Shabbat* observance, which continues even to this day, was the reading and exposition of Scripture at one's local synagogue. The English term "synagogue" is actually derived from the Greek *sunagōgē* (συναγωγή), which has a classical usage pertaining to how, "In Greek writings *a bringing together, gathering (as of fruits), a contracting; an assembling together* of men." It is more widely, of course, known in a religious context, involving "the Septuagint for קָהָל [*qahal*] and very often for עֵדָה [*eidah*]," and "*the building where those solemn Jewish assemblies are held* (Hebrew בֵּית הַכְּנֶסֶת [*beit ha'kneset*], i.e. 'the house of assembly'). Synagogues seem to date their origin from the Babylonian exile. In the time of Jesus and the apostles every town, not only in Palestine but also among the Gentiles if it contained a considerable number of Jewish inhabitants, had at least one synagogue, the larger towns several or even many" (*Thayer*).[43] Both the Jewish philosopher Philo, and the historian Josephus, from the broad First Century, testify to how reading Scripture on the Sabbath was an important practice:

> "[I]n accordance with which custom, even to this day, the Jews hold philosophical discussions on the seventh day, disputing about their national philosophy, and devoting that day to the knowledge and consideration of the subjects of natural philosophy; for as for their houses of prayer in the different cities, what are they, but schools of wisdom, and courage, and temperance, and justice, and piety, and holiness, and every virtue, by which human and divine things are appreciated, and placed upon a proper footing?" (*On the Life of Moses* 2.216).[44]

> "[F]or he {God} did not suffer the guilt of ignorance to go on without punishment, but demonstrated the law to be the best and the most necessary instruction of all others, permitting the people to stop their other employments, and to assemble

[43] Joseph H. Thayer, *Thayer's Greek-English Lexicon of the New Testament* (Peabody, MA: Hendrickson, 2003), 600.

[44] Philo Judaeus: *The Works of Philo: Complete and Unabridged*, trans. C.D. Yonge (Peabody, MA: Hendrickson, 1993), 510.

together for the hearing of the law, and learning it exactly, and this not once or twice, or oftener, but every week; which thing all the other legislators seem to have neglected" (*Against Apion* 2.175).[45]

Interestingly enough, one of the most important historical records attesting, to First Century synagogue worship and exposition of the Torah and Prophets, is the New Testament. Even with there being some sectarian differences present before the fall of the Temple in 70 C.E., it is still to be recognized how the local synagogue was a major meeting place on *Shabbat* for Jewish communities:

> "...[D]istinguishing the sabbath from the other six days of the week more than all else were, from the sixth century B.C. onward, the weekly assemblies in the local synagogues for communal worship by means of an established and steadily expanding ritual, in which the reading of the Pentateuch and selected passages from the Prophets and the expounding thereof by recognized authorities played a central role (Jos. Antiq. XVI.ii.3; Matt. 4:23; Mark 1:21-22; 6:2; Luke 4:16-21, 31-33; Acts 13:27; 15:21; 17:1-2; 18:4). Quite probably the singing or chanting of selected psalms also constituted an important part of the early synagogal sabbath ritual (cf. Ps. 92:1). There is ample ground for the assumption that prior to the destruction of the third temple by the Romans in A.D. 70 such synagogal worship was in considerable measure sectarian in character. But following this momentous event sabbath worship in the synagogue became, and has been ever since, the primary institution of Jewish ritual" (*IDB*).[46]

One of the most useful Talmudic thrusts is that whatever activity or labor can be done, before the Sabbath, may not be done on the Sabbath (b.*Pesachim* 66a-b). Most frequently, this involves not heavy labor generally, but instead various specific forms of food

---

[45] Flavius Josephus: *The Works of Josephus: Complete and Unabridged*, trans. William Whiston (Peabody, MA: Hendrickson, 1987), pp 804-805.

[46] J. Morgenstern, "Sabbath" in George Buttrick, ed. et. al., *The Interpreter's Dictionary of the Bible*, 4 vols. (Nashville: Abingdon, 1962), 4:140-141.

He goes on to state, "The Sunday-sabbath and ritual worship thereon in the church are quite obviously a part of Christianity's heritage from Judaism."

preparation (cf. m.*Shabbat* 3:4) or warming. In ancient times, food eaten on the Sabbath was prepared the day before. Obviously, in more modern times, food eaten on the Sabbath might be prepared the day before, but warmed using some form of modern technology.

There are different styles of approach witnessed throughout Judaism today toward much of the traditional *halachah* for *Shabbat*. The Orthodox Jewish community would be one of the more stringent sectors to observe the bulk of the prohibitions present during the time of Yeshua (although notably not the restrictions of the Qumran community), whereas Reform Judaism would be the most liberal, perhaps found to dismiss most of the stipulations as ancient and outdated, or reinterpret them in some way. Conservative Judaism would be found to certainly observe far less of the Mishnaic and Talmudic prohibitions than Orthodox Judaism, but far from dismissing their authority, would be more apt to interpret or adapt them in new ways for Jews in a modern setting, although many would be deemed irrelevant as they were for another time.

Welcoming and Honoring the Sabbath

It is quite common, in the Jewish tradition, to witness how the Sabbath or *Shabbat* is greeted as some kind of a queen or bride on Friday evening. It is stated in the Talmud how, "*R. Hanina would stand in his cloak on the eve of the Sabbath at sunset and exclaim,* 'Come and let us go forth to greet the Sabbath, the Queen.' *R. Yannai would put on his garments on the eve of the Sabbath and say,* 'Come, bride, come, bride'" (b.*Shabbat* 119a).[47] Recognizing how *Shabbat* is to be a memorial of the Exodus from Egypt, Ruth Perelson observes in her book *An Invitation to Shabbat*, "For many poor people, Shabbat was the one bright spot in an otherwise bleak existence, the one time each week a man was a king and a woman was a queen, no matter how humble his or her surroundings. In each generation, Shabbat continues to remind us on a regular basis of our roots and of our covenant with God."[48]

---

[47] *The Babylonian Talmud: A Translation and Commentary.*

[48] Ruth Perelson, *An Invitation to Shabbat: A Beginner's Guide to Weekly Celebration* (New York: UAHC Press, 1997), 7.

On the evening that opens the Sabbath, *Erev Shabbat* (עֶרֶב שַׁבָּת), the traditional feature in Jewish homes is the dinner table, as the Sabbath meal tends to be a unique gathering of all members of the family, to focus on God and fellowship with each other. A wide amount of preparation will go into the Sabbath evening, involving typical activities such as cooking and cleaning house, but also preparing for guests, and often making sure that the best is ready for this sacred time. When *Erev Shabbat* begins, there is traditional liturgy that is recited, sanctifying the time to the Lord, praising God for His provision, and a mutual blessing of family members such as husband and wife one to another, but most especially of parents to their children. Specific rituals and customs are observed, notably including the lighting of *Shabbat* candles, partaking of wine and bread with the *kiddush* and *challah*, and frequently also a traditional handwashing.[49]

Shabbat begins with **the kindling of Sabbath lights,** in the form of candles today (m.*Shabbat* 2:1),[50] which in the Orthodox Jewish tradition will usually take place around eighteen minutes or so before sundown. Part of lighting candles is to make the Sabbath a holy time, per the tenor of the Fourth Commandment (Exodus 20:8; Deuteronomy 5:12). Kindling a Sabbath lamp is thought to bring a degree of solace to the home (cf. b.*Shabbat* 25b). Customarily, a woman, the wife (m.*Shabbat* 2:6),[51] lights the Sabbath candles, often with some kind of hand motion over the flame, followed by a traditional blessing. As detailed by Eisenberg in the *JPS Guide to Jewish Traditions*,

"Before reciting the blessing, some women pass their hands three times over the candles to symbolically draw in the essence of light and the spirit of holiness, thus enhancing the powerful emotion of ushering in the Sabbath. It is customary for women to cover their eyes while reciting the blessing after lighting the

---

[49] A basic summary of home *Shabbat* traditions is offered in Robinson, *Essential Judaism*, pp 86-88; Eisenberg, pp 136-143.

[50] "With what do they kindle [the Sabbath light] and with what do they not kindle [it]?..." (m.*Shabbat* 2:1; Neusner, *Mishnah*, 181).

[51] "On account of three transgressions do women die in childbirth: because they are not meticulous in the laws of (1) menstrual separation, (2) in [those covering] the dough offering, and (3) in [those covering] the kindling of a lamp [for the Sabbath]" (m.*Shabbat* 2:6; Ibid., 182).

Sabbath candles. One explanation is that this enables the woman to exclude all extraneous thoughts and concentrate her full attention on the words she is saying...Covering her eyes permits the woman to delay (until after finishing the blessing) the spiritually elevating experience of gazing on the glowing light of the Sabbath candles."[52]

Kiddush (קִדּוּשׁ), the customary blessing of the wine and bread, before the Sabbath meal begins, is taken from the Hebrew *qadosh* (קָדוֹשׁ), "holy" or "sanctified." This tradition is taken from Tanach sentiments such as Isaiah 58:13, "call[ing] the sabbath a delight, the holy *day* of the LORD honorable," as well as Psalm 104:15, "wine to gladden the human heart...and bread to strengthen the human heart" (NRSV). Among Sephardic Jews, the blessings of *kiddush* are normally stated while all are standing up at the dinner table, whereas among Ashkenazic Jews, it is more common for people to be seated.[53] While any kind of kosher wine could be used, it is frequent for a sweet wine to be employed, although grape juice can also be used. The bread called ***challah*** (חַלָּה), is derived from "*the priest's share of the dough...*the quantity to be set aside for the priest" (*Jastrow*),[54] with two loaves often representative of the double portion of manna that the Ancient Israelites were to have (Exodus 16:22-26). Some of the key significance of *challah* is summarized by the *JPS Guide to Jewish Traditions:*

> "For each Sabbath meal, two whole loaves of bread (challah) are placed on the table and covered with a cloth. These are reminiscent either of the double portion of manna that fell on Friday and sustained the Israelites over the Sabbath or of the two rows (12 loaves) of the showbread (*lechem panim* [לֶחֶם פָּנִים]) eaten on the Sabbath by the *Kohanim* [priests] (Exod. 25:30). The Hebrew word '*challah*' is mentioned in the Bible (Num. 15:20) as the small portion of dough (1/24 for an individual; 1/48 for a baker) that was to be set aside when baking bread and then offered to the *Kohanim* in the Temple. Because *Kohanim* can no longer observe the laws of priestly purity and thus are disqualified from eating anything related to a holy sacrifice, in observant households (and kosher bakeries)

---

[52] Eisenberg, 137.

[53] Ibid., 140.

[54] Marcus Jastrow, *Dictionary of the Targumim, Talmud Bavli, Talmud Yerushalmi, and Midrashic Literature* (New York: Judaica Treasury, 2004), 465.

> where bread is baked, an olive-size challah portion is now thrown into the fire and burned. According to the Mishnah, Jews are responsible for separating the challah portion when baking bread from at least three pounds of flour of any of the five grains—wheat, barley, spelt, oats, and rye (Hal. 1:1).
>
> "....The Sabbath challot are usually covered with a decorative cloth, a symbol of the layer of dew that protected the manna in the wilderness. Covering the challah also prevents it from being 'slighted' by having its blessing preceded by the *Kiddush* over wine—for if bread is served at a meal, at all other times the blessing over it takes precedence...Another explanation of this practice relates to the traditional likening of the Sabbath to a bride. Just as the bridal veil is removed after reciting the blessings under the wedding canopy, so the 'veil' of the challot is lifted after their blessings have concluded and before the bread is cut...Because the dinner table is considered to be symbolic of the altar in the Temple (Ber. 55a),[55] where all was brought with all offerings, the custom developed of sprinkling salt on the challah to commemorate the sacrificial system."[56]

As a home dinner, there are a wide variety of traditional Jewish recipes, seen in both Ashkenazic and Sephardic Jewish homes.[57] Given the Talmudic dictum (b.*Shabbat* 119a), about a special spice to be used for *Shabbat* (which is actually *Shabbat*), it is hardly a surprise why many Jewish dishes served for *Erev Shabbat* may include various special and unique spices,[58] or at the very least, some sort of significant preparation, distinction, and ornateness. It is also most traditional for the *Erev Shabbat* meal to frequently, or even always, include fish.[59] (Consult the related publication,

---

[55] "For it is written, 'The altar of wood three cubits high... and he said to me, This is the table that is before the Lord' (Eze. 41:22). The verse begins by referring to the altar and concludes by referring to a table. *Both R. Yohanan and R. Eleazar say,* 'So long as the house of the sanctuary stood, the altar atoned for Israel. Now a person's table atones for him'" (b.*Berachot* 55a; *The Babylonian Talmud: A Translation and Commentary*).

[56] Eisenberg, pp 141-142.

[57] Consult Perelson, pp 15-19 for some recipe ideas.

[58] Shimon Finkelman, *Shabbos: The Sabbath—Its Essence and Significance* (Brooklyn: Mesorah Publications, 1990), 105.

[59] Ibid, pp 143-144.

Shabbat Service for Messianic Believers, which includes an example of a Messianic-adapted customary home order of service.)

While the *Erev Shabbat* dinner tends to get the most amount of attention for preparation and consumption, it is traditional for three meals to actually be eaten in association with *Shabbat* (b.*Shabbat* 117a),[60] with additional meals to occur after the morning *Shabbat* service, and another meal to occur before the close of the Sabbath in the late afternoon.[61] One custom of note is how the *Erev Shabbat* meal should be spurred on by eating sparingly the day before: "'A man should not eat on the eve of the Sabbath from afternoon onwards, so that he should be hungry at the start of the Sabbath,' the words of R. Judah" (t.*Berachot* 5:1).[62] *The Oxford Dictionary of the Jewish Religion* details a variety of additional *Shabbat* practices that are customary, often to the Orthodox community, but also adapted in various degrees by Conservative and Reform Jews:

> "Essentially, the Sabbath is a day of physical rest and spiritual joy, centered around the twin poles of home and synagogue...As the men leave for synagogue for the evening service...the women recite a special blessing over the Sabbath candles...Upon his return, the husband blesses his wife...and the children...Then the *Qiddush prayer, sanctifying the Sabbath day, is recited over wine and the *Birkat ha-Motsi' is received over two loaves of bread (*ḥallah*), which recall the two portions of manna gathered by the Israelites on the Sabbath eve. The festive meal is punctuated with the singing of Sabbath **zemirot*. At the conclusion of the meal, the *Birkat ha-Mazon is said. In non-Orthodox homes, the Sabbath meal may be eaten before the family goes to a late synagogue service. It is a

---

[60] "How many meals is a person required to eat on the Sabbath? Three. R. Hidqa says, 'Four meals is a person obligated to eat on the Sabbath.' Said R. Yohanan, 'Both authorities interpret the same verse of Scripture: "And Moses said, eat that today, for today is a Sabbath to the Lord, today you shall not find it in the field" (Exo. 16:25).' *R. Hidqa takes the view that the three 'todays' are counted in addition to the meal of the prior evening, while rabbis maintain that they encompass the meal of the prior evening*" (b.*Shabbat* 117b; *The Babylonian Talmud: A Translation and Commentary*).

[61] Eisenberg, pp 142-143.

[62] Jacob Neusner, ed., *The Tosefta: Translated from the Hebrew With a New Introduction*, 2 vols. (Peabody, MA: Hendrickson, 2002), 1:29.

widespread custom to invite guests to the Sabbath meals. Marital intercourse is regarded as especially meritorious on the Sabbath eve. In general, the Sabbath should be a 'day of delight'..."[63]

While the home tends to be the focal point for Sabbath observance on Friday evening, traditions and customs vary among branches of Judaism regarding different kinds of Friday activities at one's local synagogue, with various kinds of services indeed being held. In Reform Judaism, **an *Erev Shabbat* service** may be held at the synagogue sometime after 8:00 PM, to allow for a Sabbath home dinner.[64] It is **the *Shabbat* morning service on Saturday**—often including traditional prayers, liturgy, and some kind of teaching—that most faithful Jews will attend. (Consult the related publication, ***Shabbat Service for Messianic Believers***, which includes an example of a Messianic-adapted customary order of service.)

When three stars are sighted in the sky at twilight on Saturday, *Shabbat* can be officially said to be in the process of closing. A traditional ceremony to close *Shabbat* is ***Havdallah.*** The Hebrew term *havdallah* (הַבְדָּלָה) widely means "*separation*," but also specifically involves "*Habdalah*, a formula of prayer for the exit of the Sabbath or the Festivals" (*Jastrow*).[65] The custom of *Havdallah* is witnessed in the Mishnah, in differences between the Pharisaic schools of Hillel and Shammai (m.*Berachot* 8:5).[66] The purpose of holding *Havdallah* is so that *Shabbat* can close in a similar manner to that in which it was entered. Four features of *Havdallah* that are witnessed include: (1) a blessing over wine, (2) a blessing over spices, (3) a blessing over lights, and (4) a blessing for the new

---

[63] Chaim Pearl, "Sabbath," in R.J. Zwi Werblowsky and Geoffrey Widoger, eds., *The Oxford Dictionary of the Jewish Religion* (New York and Oxford: Oxford University Press, 1997), pp 595-596.

[64] Perelson, 3; Shapiro, pp 42-43.

[65] *Jastrow*, 329.

[66] "The House of Shammai say, '[The order of the blessings at the conclusion fo the Sabbath is] lamp, meal, spices, and *habdalah*.' But the House of Hillel says, 'Lamp, spice, meal, and *habdalah*.' [The blessing over the lamp—] the House of Shammai say, 'Who created the light of the fire.' But the House of Hillel say, 'Who creates the light of the fire'" (m.*Berachot* 8:5; Tzvee Zahavy and Alan J. Avery-Peck, trans., in Neusner, *Mishnah*, 12).

week. While there is varied symbolism attached to the elements of *Havdallah*, most frequently it is recognized how smelling spices or lighting a fire, was a prohibited activity for *Shabbat*, but now is permitted with the work week getting ready to begin. *The New Encyclopedia of Judaism* includes an important summary of what is to be widely witnessed:

> {It includes a} Blessing recited at the end of the SABBATH and FESTIVALS marking the passage from a concentrated day to a routine weekday....
>
> The *havdalah* ceremony comprises four blessings: three over WINE, SPICES, and lights, and the *havdalah* blessing. In the various rites (Ashkenazi, Sephardi, and Yemenite), the blessings themselves are almost identical, the lead phrase being *kos yeshu'ot essa* ("I will lift the cup of salvation")....
>
> Although wine is the preferred beverage for the blessing, if none is available, other liquids, except water, may be used.
>
> It is now customary to use aromatic spices for the second blessing, but until the 12th century plants such as myrtle (*hadas*) were used. In some Sephardi and Oriental communities sweet-smelling plants are still used. They recite the alternate benedictions on *asté vesamim* ("fragrant trees" or "plants") alongside the more common phrase, used by both Sephardim and Ashkenazim, *miné vsamim* ("kinds of aromatics"). The origin of this blessing is unknown. Some...attribute it to the ancient custom, predating Mishnaic times, of burning aromatic plants at the end of a meal to give a pleasant fragrance to the dining room. As this could not be done on the Sabbath, a blessing over spices was instituted.
>
> The *havdalah* spices are often kept in a special container called a *besamim* box or *hadas*. The containers, first noted in a literary source in the 15th century, come in a wide variety of shapes, such as towers, fish, and flowers, and are made of silver, wood, and other materials (see SPICEBOX).
>
> The *havdalah* candle has more than one wick, as there has to be a combination of at least two flames, stemming from the plural form "lights" used in the blessing (*Boré me'oré ha-esh*, "who creates the lights of the fire"). The candle often has six wicks and is made of interwoven strands in colorful combinations. The blessing signifies that kindling, traditionally prohibited on the Sabbath, is once again permitted on the weekday....

> A variety of customs are associated with *havdalah*, from filling the cup to overflowing and extinguishing the candle in wine poured from the cup to dipping one's fingers in the wine and putting drops on the forehead or in the pockets. It is customary to extend one's fingers or look at one's nails with the blessing over the light....Each community has its own rules regarding the drinking of the wine cup, the inhaling of the aroma of the spices, whether the *havdalah* is recited sitting or standing, and so on.
>
> REFORM JUDAISM has an alternative *havdalah* service incorporating additional readings with the traditional blessings, and it also uses the occasion for various expressions of religious creativity, such as song, dance, etc.[67]

Shabbat in the More Modern Period

Observance of the seventh-day Sabbath or *Shabbat* is something that Jewish people, faithful to God's Torah and to their ancestral heritage, have kept in various forms or fashions, across the centuries to the present. For those such as the Orthodox, *Shabbat* begins eighteen minutes before sundown on Friday evening; for those such as the Reform, *Shabbat* begins when everyone can sit down at the dinner table on Friday evening.[68] Certainly, ranging from issues such as finding oneself living in the modern West, with Twentieth and Twenty-First Century levels of technology and convenience—to living in the Jewish State of Israel, with a religiously-influenced civil law—there are many discussions, debates, and diverse forms of Sabbath application to be seen.

One of the most highlighted components of Sabbath observance in the modern period tends to surround the difference of approach to driving cars on *Shabbat* and the usage of modern electrical devices—and whether they fall within the Exodus 35:3 prohibition of kindling a fire. *EJ* details some of the main differences of allowance between the major branches of contemporary Judaism:

> "Modern inventions have produced a host of new questions regarding Sabbath observance. Orthodox Judaism forbids travel by automobile on the Sabbath, Reform Judaism permits

---

[67] "Havdalah," in *The New Encyclopedia of Judaism*, pp 349-350.

[68] Perelson, pp 2-3.

> it. Conservative Judaism has differing views on this question, but generally permits travel by automobile on the Sabbath solely for the purpose of attending synagogue. The basic legal question regarding the switching on of electric lights is whether the noncombustive type of burning produced by electricity falls under the prohibition of making a fire or any of the other [traditional] prohibitions...Orthodox Jews refrain from the use of electrical appliances on the Sabbath, with the exception of the refrigerator, which may be open and closed on the grounds that any electrical current produced in the process is incidental and without express intention. It has, however, become the practice for observant Jews to use electrical appliances on the Sabbath which are operated by time switches set before the Sabbath. In Israel, on religious kibbutzim, the same procedure is used to milk the cows on the Sabbath. Israel also has local bylaws forbidding certain activities on the Sabbath. There is, however, no comprehensive law covering the whole country. Thus, whereas the public transport does not operate on the Sabbath in Jerusalem and in Tel Aviv, it does in Haifa. Except for specifically non-Jewish sections of the country, the Sabbath is the official day of rest on which all business and stores must close."[69]

So much of the discussion over "Do not light a fire in any of your dwellings on the Sabbath day" (Exodus 35:3, NIV) will concern a contrast and comparison on *what it actually took* to kindle or light a fire in the Ancient Near East for Ancient Israel—and what it takes today. Is it or is it not "work" to flip a light switch, via an ongoing "fire" provided by a coal, petroleum, or nuclear power plant? Is it or is it not "work" to turn the keys of a car ignition—versus how in ancient times a fire could only start via some semi-intense human labor of striking a flint over and over? Is it or is it not even "work" to initiate a fire by striking a match or flipping a lighter?[70]

---

[69] Louis Jacobs, "Sabbath: Laws and Customs of the Sabbath," in Encyclopaedia Judaica. MS Windows 9x. Brooklyn: Judaica Multimedia (Israel) Ltd, 1997.

Judith Shulevitz, *The Sabbath World: Glimpses of a Different Order of Time* (New York: Random House, 2010), pp 44-46 for some of the main features of Sabbath keeping in modern Israel, in particular in Jerusalem, as well as some of the controversy that it has stirred.

[70] Much of this is evaluated further on, in "Being Realistic About Shabbat," by J.K. McKee.

The major thrust to be sure, of course, is how *Shabbat* is intended to be—whether witnessed in Holy Scripture or mainline Jewish tradition and custom—**a special time committed unto the Lord.** Eisenberg addresses in the *JPS Guide to Jewish Traditions*,

"According to Samuel Raphael Hirsch, the prohibition of creative activity on the Sabbath is a critical acknowledgment of God as the Creator. Human beings are permitted to rule over the natural world for six days by divine decree, but on the seventh day they are forbidden to make anything for their own purpose. In effect, on the Sabbath humans relinquish their temporary control over the world and return it to the ultimate Creator of all."[71]

To be sure, while committing one's observance of the Sabbath unto the Lord and to His sovereignty is something positive to be embraced, to what degree does the Prophet Isaiah's admonition, "if you honor it and go not your ways nor look to your affairs, nor strike bargains" (58:13, NJPS), specifically apply? It should hardly be a surprise how there is not uniformity regarding how *Shabbat*-honoring is not present in contemporary Judaism. While the Sabbath has been something recognized as important among the branches of mainstream Judaism, varied levels of application and emphasis on *Shabbat* being an *oneg* (עֹנֶג) or "delight" (Isaiah 58:13)[72] are present. *The Oxford Dictionary of the Jewish Religion* entry on "Sabbath" offers a fair presentation of the different approaches present in contemporary Judaism:

> All streams in Judaism have stressed the centrality of the Sabbath. For several decades the REFORM movement distanced itself from traditional observances and practices, including attempts to transfer the Sabbath to Sunday (an idea which did not succeed). Today, in both CONSERVATIVE and Reform Judaism the main weekly synagogal service is held on Friday night and/or Sabbath morning. Lighting CANDLES in the home and

[71] Eisenberg, 128.

[72] In today's broad Messianic movement, the noun *oneg* is typically used to describe the post-service refreshments or mealtime following an *Erev Shabbat* or *Shabbat* service. This tends to be an excellent community-builder for Messianic assemblies and fellowships, as it will stimulate interaction among brothers and sisters.

At the publishers' own local Messianic congregation, Eitz Chaim of Richardson, TX, there is an *oneg* lunch following the morning *Shabbat* service.

> reciting the KIDDUSH are widely practiced private rituals. Abstention from commercial activity and gainful employment are encouraged, as is dedication of the Sabbath day to spiritual and contemplative endeavors. Although Reform Judaism does not require fulfillment of all the traditional commandments as defined in the *halakhah*, it stresses the fundamental goals of *kedushah* (holiness), *menuḥuah* (rest), and *oneg* (joy) in celebration of the Sabbath day. The specific form of expression given to these values is a matter of contemporary individual interpretation and not merely the adoption or even adaptation of historical expressions and forms. Conservative, Reform, and Reconstructionist synagogues have experimented with and often adopted creative innovations in their Sabbath services.[73]

Reform Judaism, the most open and liberal of all the mainstream branches of Judaism,[74] permits activities such as circumcision (Genesis 17:11-12; cf. John 7:22), prohibits weddings, and prohibits funerals and cemetery visits on *Shabbat*.[75] Among those who are more Centrist to traditional, it is to be recognized how those hallowing and sanctifying *Shabbat*, have to expel some effort or "work" during the week, in order to make the Sabbath a special time. This not only concerns facilitating the time for *Shabbat*, so that all work- and job-related responsibilities have ceased—but also so that the key instructions from the Torah can be honored. Dresner offers some key application, from a Conservative Jewish standpoint, of what it means to sanctify *Shabbat:*

> What do we mean by "keeping the Sabbath holy"?...[D]rawing upon the Tradition, we may say that to keep the Sabbath *(kadosh)*, includes, in addition to abstaining from work, basically the following:
>
> 1) Cleaning, arranging and adorning one's home, one's wardrobe and one's person—and preparing special meals—in advance of the Sabbath in honor of the Sabbath.

---

[73] Pearl, "Sabbath," in *The Oxford Dictionary of the Jewish Religion*, 667.

[74] Consult Shapiro, pp 95-99 for a basic list of Reform Jewish prohibited activities for *Shabbat*.

[75] Ibid., 58.

2) Providing for the needy in advance of the Sabbath; and inviting the stranger, the needy, the lonely and the troubled to share in one's Sabbath.
3) Welcoming the Sabbath with the lighting of candles and *Kiddush*, and ushering it out with *Havdalah*.
4) Studying Torah, individually or in groups.
5) Eating festive meals, wearing special clothes, taking a leisurely walk, taking special Sabbath rest.
6) Increasing one's appreciation and enjoyment of the creations of the human spirit—such as literature and song.
7) Deepening the level of love and affection, of concern and care, of sharing and understanding among members of the household and among friends.
8) Turning to God by praying the evening, morning and afternoon services (with a congregation if possible, or else privately) and by reciting the Grace before and after meals—in thankfulness and wonderment at the blessings of creation and the gift of rest; in gratitude for redemption from enslavement; in examination of conscience and request for forgiveness; in sympathy for human suffering and deprivation, and in resolve to aid in their alleviation; in renewal of the covenant-bond with the people Israel; and in petition for an increase in inner resources for living.[76]

Even with a wide number of liberal perspectives and views present in his broad-sweeping *Essential Judaism: A Complete Guide to Beliefs, Customs, and Rituals*, George Robinson is still right to emphasize how the Sabbath—especially given that common greeting *Shabbat shalom* (שַׁבָּת שָׁלוֹם)—is to be a day of significant peace. This does require those who truly intended to honor the Sabbath, to alter their orientation of one toward self-importance and self-indulgence—toward one of focusing on God and the ways of God:

"Shabbat is meant to be a day of peace, *Shabbat shalom*, the peace of the Sabbath. It offers us a chance for peace with nature, with society, and with ourselves. The prohibitions on work are designed to make us stop—if only for one day of the

[76] Dresner, pp 80-81.

> week—our relentless efforts to tame, to conquer, to subdue the earth and everything on it. The prohibition against making fire is also said by the rabbis to mean that one should not kindle the fires of controversy against one's fellow humans. And, finally, the Sabbath offers us a moment of quiet, of serenity, of self-transcendence, a moment that allows us to seek and perhaps achieve some kind of internal peace."[77]

Today's Messianic people do, on the whole, tend to have a very high appreciation level for some of the major traditions and customs observed throughout mainstream Judaism, for honoring the seventh-day Sabbath or *Shabbat*. Certainly, some fine-tuning as to the origination of many of the key, edifying traditions, and how they could be better employed, is in order. Perhaps more than anything else, what we do encounter in today's Messianic movement—given the fact that wide numbers of today's Messianic Jews, and certainly various non-Jewish Messianic Believers, have had significant experience in evangelical Christianity—is *a conscious need for us to move* from a mentality of treating *Shabbat* as some kind of "Saturday church," where we only gather to corporately worship on the seventh-day, to a time of widescale rest and refreshment (cf. Exodus 20:10; Deuteronomy 5:14). This is indeed achievable and by no means impossible, because we serve a Lord who decreed, "Take My yoke upon you and learn from Me, for I am gentle and humble in heart, and 'you will find rest for your souls' [Jeremiah 6:16]'" (Matthew 11:29, TLV).[78]

---

[77] Robinson, 84.

[78] For a further review on the significance of the seventh-day Sabbath or *Shabbat* in contemporary Judaism, it is recommended that you consult Ruth Perelson, *An Invitation to Shabbat: A Beginner's Guide to Weekly Celebration* (New York: UAHC Press, 1997), for a summary of views from Reform Judaism; Samuel H. Dresner *The Sabbath* (New York: The Burning Bush Press, 1970), for a summary of views from Conservative Judaism; and Abraham Joshua Heschel, *The Sabbath* (New York: Farrar, Straus and Giroux, 1951), for a relatively philosophical Jewish review.

Is Sunday "the Lord's Day"?

It appears on countless church bulletins, newsletters, and is frequently referred to by many Christians, both Protestants and Catholics. It is "the Lord's Day," believed to be Sunday when most Christians believe that Yeshua the Messiah (Jesus Christ) was resurrected from the dead.[1] Because of Yeshua resurrecting from the dead on this day, Christians assemble in worship, some to obey the Forth Commandment: "Remember the sabbath day, to keep it holy" (Exodus 20:8-11; Deuteronomy 5:12). Other Christians believe that the Fourth Commandment has been annulled and are of the position that they should observe Sunday, as was the pattern of the Second and Third Century Church.

We as Messianic Believers come into direct contrast with many Christians because we do not observe this "Lord's Day," as they call it. We keep the Biblical seventh-day Sabbath or *Shabbat* (שַׁבָּת), the day of rest that God established for His people going back to the start of human history (Genesis 2:3; Exodus 20:11).

Some uninformed Christians may accuse us of being legalistic about *Shabbat*, perhaps implying that because we do not assemble on Sunday, as they do, that we cannot be true Believers. (Many others simply do not understand what *Shabbat* is all about.) Various claims issued against us can be very serious because **we do believe** in the shed blood of the Messiah as being our sin covering, and that salvation comes by grace through faith. However, obeying God should come as fruit of a true conversion experience. Christians

---

[1] This chapter was originally written for *Torah In the Balance, Volume I* (Kissimmee, FL: TNN Press, 2003/2009).

who accuse Messianics who keep God's Sabbath as not being "saved" are on extremely dangerous ground—coming against things that He, not man, has established. Messianics today keep the Sabbath because Yeshua Himself did.

It has never been my position to criticize Christians unfairly or "attack back," as do some Messianics when Christians tell them that they are "trying to earn their salvation" or somehow committing sacrilege, often relating to *Shabbat*. However, we do have a very definite position on *why* we should keep the Biblical Sabbath, and not "the Lord's Day" as instituted by those who came *after* our Lord. This needs to be discussed in a fair and reasonable manner, where Messianics are given a hearing.

Let us detail what the Creator God has established for humanity, and answer some of the major claims given by Christians as to why we should not keep the Biblical Sabbath. We will examine the fact that Messiah Yeshua's atoning work does not annul the Sabbath, and why He did not break it during His ministry on Earth. We will also discuss why Sunday, or the first day, is not really "the Lord's Day."

What day has God set-apart?

When we review the account of Creation in Genesis chs. 1-2, it is very clear what day of the week our Heavenly Father has set-apart or chosen to be unique: "By the seventh day God completed His work which He had done, and He rested on the seventh day from all His work which He had done. Then God blessed the seventh day and sanctified it, because in it He rested from all His work which God had created and made" (Genesis 2:2-3).[2]

The Hebrew verb *qadash* (קָדַשׁ), translated "sanctified," appears in the Piel stem (intensive action, active voice) and means "to **proclaim a holy period**" or "to **treat someone (something) as sanctified, consecrated**" (*HALOT*).[3] In other words, it is the

[2] Some say that the Sabbath does not appear in Genesis 2:2-3, yet the verb form of *Shabbat* (שַׁבָּת), *shavat* (שָׁבַת), does appear: *v'**yishbot** b'yom ha'shevi'i* (וַיִּשְׁבֹּת בַּיּוֹם הַשְּׁבִיעִי).

Cf. Victor P. Hamilton, "שָׁבַת," in *TWOT*, 2:902-903; Ludwig Koehler and Walter Baumgartner, eds., *The Hebrew & Aramaic Lexicon of the Old Testament*, 2 vols. (Leiden, the Netherlands: Brill, 2001), 2:1407.

[3] *HALOT*, 2:1074.

seventh day, or *yom ha'shevi'i* (יוֹם הַשְּׁבִיעִי), that God has indicated as being special. The Lord "blessed the seventh day and made it holy" (Genesis 2:3, NIV). Torah commentator J.H. Hertz states that "The Creator endowed the Sabbath with a blessing which would be experienced by all who observed it. . ..It is specifically marked off as a day consecrated to God and the life of the spirit."[4] John H. Walton further remarks, "The divine Sabbath of Genesis 2 is not simply an etiology of the human Sabbath. . .Instead, the divine Sabbath is seen as the cause of the human Sabbath."[5] Those who keep the Sabbath identify with God in a very unique and significant way. Yeshua spoke of how "The sabbath was made for humankind" (Mark 2:27, NRSV), indicating how it has universal effects for all people.

The instruction to observe the Sabbath was first given in Exodus 20:8-11, as a part of the Ten Commandments:

"Remember the sabbath day, to keep it holy. Six days you shall labor and do all your work, but the seventh day is a sabbath of the LORD your God; *in it* you shall not do any work, you or your son or your daughter, your male or your female servant or your cattle or your sojourner who stays with you. For in six days the LORD made the heavens and the earth, the sea and all that is in them, and rested on the seventh day; therefore the LORD blessed the sabbath day and made it holy."

This is repeated in Deuteronomy 5:12: "Observe the sabbath day to keep it holy, as the LORD your God commanded you."

Furthermore, the Sabbath is one of the Father's *moedim* (מוֹעֲדִים) or "appointed times" in Leviticus 23: "For six days work may be done, but on the seventh day there is a sabbath of complete rest, a holy convocation. You shall not do any work; it is a sabbath to the LORD in all your dwellings" (Leviticus 23:3).

These commandments are quite straightforward when we understand them Biblically. Our Heavenly Father rested after His creative acts were finished, and He established *Shabbat* as a time of rest for His own to consider His wonders, experiencing a foretaste of a *greater rest* to come (cf. Hebrews 4:9-11). It is the day that He

---

[4] J.H. Hertz, ed., *Pentateuch & Haftorahs* (London: Soncino Press, 1960), 6.

[5] John H. Walton, *NIV Application Commentary: Genesis* (Grand Rapids: Zondervan, 2001), 153.

has set-apart and made holy, so that we might rest and rejuvenate ourselves and meditate on Him. Certainly, resting from our labors for a full day is *a good thing!* As Believers who want to focus on Messiah Yeshua, spending an entire day meditating on God's Word, worshipping Him, and fellowshipping with others is not bad!

In Exodus 31:16-17, the Lord states that keeping the Sabbath is an eternal sign between Him and His people forever: "So the sons of Israel shall observe the Sabbath [*v'shamru...et'ha'Shabbat*, וְשָׁמְרוּ. . .אֶת־הַשַּׁבָּת], to celebrate the sabbath throughout their generations as a perpetual covenant [*l'dorotam b'rit olam*, לְדֹרֹתָם בְּרִית עוֹלָם]. It is a sign between Me and the sons of Israel forever; for in six days the LORD made heaven and earth, but on the seventh day He ceased *from labor*, and was refreshed."

The Hebrew term used for "sign" in this passage is *ot* (אוֹת), and it means "*sign, pledge token*," and "*signs, miracles*, as pledges or attestations of divine presence & interposition" (*BDB*).[6] Those who keep *Shabbat* are distinguished and set-apart from the rest of the world, because unlike the world—which continues to conduct in business and hectic work—by keeping *Shabbat* we can identify ourselves with the God of Israel and with His practices. *It is a distinct sign manifest to others on a regular basis that we are His*, and that we have placed ourselves in His care.

Many of us who observe *Shabbat*, though, are also separated from other "Believers" from time to time, because it can be sadly observed that a few of those who follow the Lord's commandments in this regard can be criticized and harassed. This often comes from people who have not been sufficiently taught about what the Sabbath actually is from the Scriptures.[7]

Shabbat was made by God to be a *b'rit olam* (בְּרִית עוֹלָם), an "eternal" or "perpetual covenant" between Him and His people.

---

[6] Francis Brown, S.R. Driver, and Charles A. Briggs, *Hebrew and English Lexicon of the Old Testament* (Oxford: Clarendon Press, 1979), 16.

[7] Remarking on Hebrews 4:1, Tim Hegg indicates that "The answer to the question of why. . .Christian theologians and teachers have neglected the theology of 'rest' may simply lie in the fact that the Church jettisoned Sabbath. With Sabbath no longer part of the Christian culture and practice, the emphasis shifted from 'rest' to 'work'. In this scenario, biblical 'rest' becomes entirely allegorized as symbolic of eternity *and therefore of no current consequence*" (*Commentary on the Epistle to the Hebrews* [Author, n.d.], 61).

Some have tried to argue that the context of *olam* (עוֹלָם), "*for ever, always,*" "*continuous existence,*" "*everlasting covenant,*" "*indefinite, unending future,*" "*everlastingness, eternity*"—when we survey the array of possible applications in *BDB*[8]—meant that one day the Sabbath commandment would outlive itself.[9] But the Lord very clearly says that *Shabbat* is part of His covenant, and if *Shabbat* were done away with, it means that God is not true to His covenants. ***Eternal means eternal***, and being an ordinance existing from Creation, the Sabbath would be a very difficult observance to entirely revoke and abolish. Certainly, while the Sabbath teaches us things *beyond* just a single day of human rest in a week on Planet Earth (cf. Colossians 2:17), one cannot hope to understand greater realities beyond this dimension, without actually first participating in a weekly *Shabbat* rest.

Exodus 31:18 further says that "When He had finished speaking with him upon Mount Sinai, He gave Moses the two tablets of the testimony, tablets of stone, written by the finger of God." The Sabbath commandment, a major sign that is to distinguish His people from the world, was written into stone with the *etzba Elohim* (אֶצְבַּע אֱלֹהִים) or "the finger of God." Considering that the Sabbath commandment was written with the Lord's very "finger," it is important that we take notice. Truly, those who would say that something written with the Heavenly Father's finger, is now done away, are treading on dangerous ground. (No one in his right mind argues that the Sixth Commandment, the prohibition against murder, has been done away!)

There is one argument that many Christians give that only today's Messianics can easily answer. It is commonly said that the *Shabbat* commandment was only given to Israel and thus does not apply to "the Church." These Christians say they are not required to keep it, as it was something only for the Jews. But non-Jewish Believers in Yeshua are a part of the Commonwealth of Israel (Ephesians 2:11-12) or the Israel of God (Galatians 6:16). They "are

---

[8] *BDB*, pp 761-762.

[9] Sadly, misunderstanding the significance of the Sabbath can even extend to Messianic Jewish Bible teachers, and is not constrained to Christian pastors alone. See the comments of Arnold G. Fructenbaum, *Israelology: The Missing Link in Systematic Theology* (Tustin, CA: Ariel Ministries, 1996), pp 594-595, 601.

fellow heirs and fellow members of the body" (Ephesians 3:6) along with the Jewish people. Our Heavenly Father has only one chosen assembly: the community of Israel of which ***all Believers*** are a part. Thus, *Shabbat* should be kept by all Believers. It is certainly something that can bless those who take a hold of it, and honor the Lord by resting and meeting with Him.

Is the Sabbath a burden?

In discussing what *Shabbat* actually is, many have the false idea that the Sabbath is to be a forced time of "unwork," burdensome and legalistic. Unfortunately, these ideas concerning *Shabbat* do not necessarily come from Scripture, but rather from various concepts of modern-day Orthodox Judaism— perhaps not even the Judaism of Yeshua's day.

Many of our Jewish brethren, while serious about keeping the Sabbath—which is good—have unfortunately made it burdensome, imposing many extra-Biblical regulations. There are, in fact, thirty-nine specific types of work prohibited by the Mishnah (m.*Shabbat* 7:2). These prohibitions were originally put in place by the Jewish Rabbis to mimic the type of work that was used by the Ancient Israelites in the construction of the Tabernacle. Many of these things clearly do classify as laborious work and should not be practiced on the Sabbath, and they can aid us when trying to discern something as "work." However, some of these things may be contested as being classified as laborious. In time, these man-made rules expanded the meaning of *Shabbat* beyond the original intentions of God, and these thirty-nine abstentions led to many more customs and traditions being added:

> The generative categories of acts of labor [prohibited on the Sabbath] are forty less one: (1) he who sews, (2) ploughs, (3) reaps, (4) binds sheaves, (5) threshes, (6) winnows, (7) selects [fit from unfit produce or crops], (8) grinds, (9) sifts, (10) kneads, (11) bakes; (12) he who shears wool, (13) washes it, (14) beats it, (15) dyes it; (16) spins, (17) weaves, (18) makes two loops, (19) weaves two threads, (20) separates two threads; (21) ties, (22) unties, (23) sews two stitches, (24) tears in order to sew two stitches; (25) he who traps a deer, (26) slaughters it, (27) flays it, (28) salts it, (29) cures its hide, (30) scrapes it, and (31) cuts it up; (32) he who writes two letters, (33) erases two

> letters in order to write two letters; (34) he who builds, (35) tears down; (36) he who puts out a fire, (37) kindles a fire; (38) he who hits with a hammer; (39) he who transports an object from one domain to another—lo, these are the forty generative acts of labor less one (m.*Shabbat* 7:2).[10]

But what does Scripture *specifically* say about how we are to keep the Sabbath day? Is the Sabbath truly a "burden"? The Pentateuch first records,

> "For six days work may be done, but on the seventh day there is a sabbath of complete rest, holy to the LORD; whoever does any work on the sabbath day shall surely be put to death" (Exodus 31:15).

> "For six days work may be done, but on the seventh day you shall have a holy *day*, a sabbath of complete rest to the LORD; whoever does any work on it shall be put to death" (Exodus 35:2).

These two verses listed above say that those who work on *Shabbat* will be condemned to death. As far as we know, when these commandments were observed, those who violated the Sabbath in ancient times were put to death.

We do know that now Messiah Yeshua has taken the death penalty for these sins away by His atoning work on the cross (Colossians 2:14), and so ***we will not***, of course, demand the death of those who do not take this commandment seriously. However, as it may be observed—conceptually as "life" is communion with God and "death" is separation from Him—by failing to properly keep *Shabbat* we can be separate from the Father and be unable to properly commune with Him. We do not get to participate in all the things that He has intended for us. But, if we keep *Shabbat* and rest from our labors, then we *can* meditate and commune with Him in a very full and meaningful way—certainly something none of us should have a problem with.

But is the Sabbath a "burden" as some Christians believe?

Here are a collection of specific admonitions in the Tanach as they relate to properly keeping *Shabbat*:

---

[10] Neusner, *Mishnah*, pp 187-188.

1. The Seventh day is the Sabbath, requiring a suspension of all labor:
"[B]ut the seventh day is a sabbath of the LORD your God; *in it* you shall not do any work, you or your son or your daughter, your male or your female servant or your cattle or your sojourner who stays with you" (Exodus 20:10).

2. The Sabbath is to be a holy convocation:
"For six days work may be done, but on the seventh day there is a sabbath of complete rest, a holy convocation. You shall not do any work; it is a sabbath to the LORD in all your dwellings" (Leviticus 23:3).

3. Work is to be done in the first six days of the week:
"Six days you shall labor and do all your work" (Exodus 20:9).

4. The Sabbath is to be a day of complete rest:
"You shall work six days, but on the seventh day you shall rest; *even* during plowing time and harvest you shall rest" (Exodus 34:21).

5. Fire shall not be kindled on the Sabbath:
"You shall not kindle a fire in any of your dwellings on the sabbath day" (Exodus 35:3).

6. On the Sabbath, we are to remember that the Ancient Israelites were once slaves in Egypt:
"You shall remember that you were a slave in the land of Egypt, and the LORD your God brought you out of there by a mighty hand and by an outstretched arm; therefore the LORD your God commanded you to observe the sabbath day" (Deuteronomy 5:15).

7. We are not to be concerned about our own carnal pleasures:
"If because of the sabbath, you turn your foot from doing your *own* pleasure on My holy day, and call the Sabbath a delight, the holy *day* of the LORD honorable, and honor it, desisting from your *own* ways, from seeking your *own* pleasure and speaking *your own* word, then you will take delight in the LORD, and I will make you ride on the heights of the earth; and I will

> feed you *with* the heritage of Jacob your father, for the mouth of the LORD has spoken" (Isaiah 58:13-14).

> **8. Conducting in business is prohibited on the Sabbath:**
> "As for the peoples of the land who bring wares or any grain on the sabbath day to sell, we will not buy from them on the sabbath or a holy day; and we will forego *the crops* the seventh year and the exaction of every debt" (Nehemiah 10:31).

Many of these admonitions are not burdensome in the least, especially for those who want to obey God with an open heart. Abstaining from all labors, remembering what God has done for His people in the past, and not conducting in business for an entire day are *good things*—not to be looked down upon. The Sabbath is *a special gift* from our Heavenly Father to His people, that we might spend a day in complete rest and meditation on Him. Those who believe that keeping *Shabbat* and dedicating this day entirely unto Him is gross legalistic error, probably have selfish motivations. Such people could probably also be led to believe that studying the Bible regularly or in any kind of detail, or committing oneself to a disciplined prayer life, is "legalistic."

Certainly the Biblical commandments listed relating to keeping the Sabbath are interpreted differently among Messianics. We trust that you will be guided by the Holy Spirit in determining a proper application for your life's circumstances. But the general consensus should be that *Shabbat* is to be a day of abstention from work and rest in Him.

The Messiah Observed the Sabbath

Many Believers today eagerly wish to follow the example of our Messiah Yeshua. Following what our Savior did is imperative, as we live in a world that is greatly deteriorating because we have failed to follow the Bible. So if we want to follow the example of Yeshua, are we to keep the Sabbath? Consider the following scenes from the Gospels:

> "They went into Capernaum; and immediately on the Sabbath He entered the synagogue and *began* to teach. They were amazed at His teaching; for He was teaching them as *one* having authority, and not as the scribes" (Mark 1:21-22).

> "When the Sabbath came, He began to teach in the synagogue; and the many listeners were astonished, saying, 'Where did this man *get* these things, and what is *this* wisdom given to Him, and such miracles as these performed by His hands?'" (Mark 6:2).

> "And He came to Nazareth, where He had been brought up; and as was His custom, He entered the synagogue on the Sabbath, and stood up to read. And the book of the prophet Isaiah was handed to Him. And He opened the book and found the place where it was written, 'THE SPIRIT OF THE LORD IS UPON ME, BECAUSE HE ANOINTED ME TO PREACH THE GOSPEL TO THE POOR. HE HAS SENT ME TO PROCLAIM RELEASE TO THE CAPTIVES, AND RECOVERY OF SIGHT TO THE BLIND, TO SET FREE THOSE WHO ARE OPPRESSED, TO PROCLAIM THE FAVORABLE YEAR OF THE LORD.' And He closed the book, gave it back to the attendant and sat down; and the eyes of all in the synagogue were fixed on Him. And He began to say to them, 'Today this Scripture has been fulfilled in your hearing'" (Luke 4:16-21; cf. Isaiah 61:1-2; 58:6).

These verses all attest to the miraculous teaching ability of the Messiah on *Shabbat*, and the declaration of His fulfillment of Biblical prophecy as He quoted Isaiah 61:1-2 from the scroll:

"And He came down to Capernaum, a city of Galilee, and He was teaching them on the Sabbath; and they were amazed at His teaching, for His message was with authority" (Luke 4:31-32).

From these selections, it is clear that Yeshua kept the Sabbath. In fact, *Shabbat* is connected with Yeshua's authoritative teaching ability, as on *Shabbat* those assembling in Jewish synagogues would listen to and discuss the Torah and the Prophets. If we wish to enrich our spiritual lives, should we do the same as well? These parts of the Bible are *greatly overlooked* by Christians at large, who often misunderstand the teachings of God's Torah, because they may never read it on a consistent basis (cf. Acts 15:21). On *Shabbat*, Messianic Believers assemble with one another, discuss the Torah and the Prophets—and uplift and praise our Messiah Yeshua—seeing the richness of these texts in light of the Apostolic Scriptures (New Testament)!

Did Yeshua break the Sabbath?

Some Christians are of the position that our Messiah Yeshua, the sinless Lamb of God and perfect sacrifice for our sin, actually broke the Sabbath. This is a serious claim because if He broke the Sabbath and if He sinned, then perhaps Yeshua could not be the Messiah and His sacrifice could not atone for our sin—which 1 John 3:4 tells us is lawlessness or disobedience to God's Torah.

There are two specific instances to discuss that some Christians believe give reference to the Messiah breaking *Shabbat*.

The first claim usually given to prove that the Messiah "broke the Sabbath" is seen when His Disciples were plucking grain in the fields (Matthew 12:1-8; Mark 2:23-28; Luke 6:1-5):

"At that time Yeshua went through the grainfields on the Sabbath, and His disciples became hungry and began to pick the heads *of grain* and eat. But when the Pharisees saw *this*, they said to Him, 'Look, Your disciples do what is not lawful to do on a Sabbath.' But He said to them, 'Have you not read what David did when he became hungry, he and his companions, how he entered the house of God, and they ate the consecrated bread, which was not lawful for him to eat nor for those with him, but for the priests alone?'" (Matthew 12:1-4).

Those who tell us from these verses that Yeshua broke the Sabbath usually quote the Pharisees who said, "Why are you doing what is not permitted to be done on the Sabbath days?" (Luke 6:2, Amplified Bible). The Complete Jewish Bible translates this as, "Why are you violating *Shabbat*?" While Yeshua is not picking the heads of grain, His Disciples are, and this reflects back on Him as their Teacher and Rabbi.

It is important for us to first note that there is no specific commandment in the Torah that forbids picking heads of grain on the Sabbath. The Greek *exesti* (ἔξεστι) correctly means, "*it is allowed, it is in one's power, is possible*" (*LS*),[11] not always referring to something in the Pentateuch itself. The Mishnah includes two types of work on the Sabbath that were prohibited by

---

[11] *LS*, 273.

The full clause in Luke 6:2 is *ti poieite ho ouk exestin tois sabbasin* (τί ποιεῖτε ὃ οὐκ ἔξεστιν τοῖς σάββασιν), also rendered as "Why do you do what is forbidden on the Sabbath?" (*Lattimore*).

Rabbis in Yeshua's day, which He could have been accused of breaking: reaping and threshing (m.*Shabbat* 7:2). Those holding a rigid interpretation of the Oral Law would have immediately accused Yeshua of doing something that was not permitted on the Sabbath. However, Luke 6:2 notably records, "But some of the Pharisees said."[12] The text does not indicate that this was a position held by *all* of the Pharisees. Placing this passage in its appropriate historical context is imperative.[13]

Secondly, in His response to these Pharisees, Yeshua gives the example of David and his men eating the consecrated bread that was only reserved for the priests to be eaten. This is recorded in 1 Samuel 21:3-4, 6:

"'Now therefore, what do you have on hand? Give me five loaves of bread, or whatever can be found.' The priest answered David and said, 'There is no ordinary bread on hand, but there is consecrated bread; if only the young men have kept themselves from women'. . .So the priest gave him consecrated *bread*; for there was no bread there but the bread of the Presence which was removed from before the LORD, in order to put hot bread *in its place* when it was taken away."

In the example given from the Tanach regarding David and his men, it is important to recognize how the priest provided them with food from the Bread of the Presence, which was only permitted for the priests to eat. The Torah says in Leviticus 24:9 that this bread "shall be for Aaron and his sons, and they shall eat it in a holy place; for it is most holy to him from the LORD's offerings by fire, *his* portion forever." However, because they were hungry and required sustenance, the priest gave them this bread.

Eating something to provide sustenance and thus maintain one's physical life falls into a category that the Rabbis of Judaism call *Pikku'ach Nefesh* or Regard for Human Life. It is based on Leviticus 19:16: "neither shalt thou stand idly by the blood of thy neighbour" (1917 JPS). The *ArtScroll Chumash* commentary states, "If someone's life is in danger, you must try to save him."[14] In

---

[12] Grk. *tines de tōn Pharisaiōn eipan* (τινὲς δὲ τῶν Φαρισαίων εἶπαν).

[13] In all likelihood, the Pharisees Yeshua encountered here were of the more conservative and stringent School of Shammai.

[14] Nosson Scherman, ed., *ArtScroll Chumash, Stone Edition* (Brooklyn: Mesorah Publications, Ltd., 2000), 661.

regard to the Sabbath the principle of *Pikku'ach Nefesh* has often been taken to mean that any work that is required to save a person's life takes precedence over the ritual *Shabbat* commandments of the Torah. (This is the reason why in the modern State of Israel today, doctors, police, and the military are permitted to work on *Shabbat*.)

Yeshua's example of David being fed by the Bread of the Presence was poignant in that the priest followed Leviticus 19:16 by providing needed sustenance to David and his party. And, His Disciples were likewise only providing for themselves the necessary food for survival. Yeshua's Disciples plucking heads of grain on the Sabbath was well-permitted within the larger theological construct of First Century Judaism, but was probably not liked by a few.

Another example often used by those who say that Yeshua broke *Shabbat* comes from John 5:6-18, where He healed a sick man on the Sabbath. Yeshua then commanded him to pick up his pallet and walk:

"When Yeshua saw him lying *there*, and knew that he had already been a long time *in that condition*, He said to him, 'Do you wish to get well?' The sick man answered Him, 'Sir, I have no man to put me into the pool when the water is stirred up, but while I am coming, another steps down before me.' Yeshua said to him, 'Get up, pick up your pallet and walk.' Immediately the man became well, and picked up his pallet and *began* to walk. Now it was the Sabbath on that day" (John 5:6-9).

In these verses, we can most certainly see application of *Pikku'ach Nefesh*. Yeshua was saving the life of a person by healing him on the Sabbath. In response to this, we see the reaction of some of the Jews watching this: "It is the Sabbath, and it is not permissible for you to carry your pallet" (John 5:10). These Pharisees were dismayed that the man would carry his pallet on *Shabbat*, because they probably believed that it was in violation of Nehemiah 13:19-20:

"It came about that just as it grew dark at the gates of Jerusalem before the sabbath, I commanded that the doors should be shut and that they should not open them until after the sabbath. Then I stationed some of my servants at the gates *so that* no load would enter on the sabbath day. Once or twice the traders and merchants of every kind of merchandise spent the night outside Jerusalem."

These verses indicate that it was prohibited for loads to be carried on the Sabbath, but specifically loads relating to business and commerce. These loads were being carried into Jerusalem for buying and selling on *Shabbat*, which is why Jerusalem's gates were closed. Without a doubt, many Pharisees considered this to be a "burden" or *massa* (מַשָּׂא), which means "load, burden, lifting, bearing, tribute" (*BDB*),[15] including pallets. The Septuagint translates *massa* as *bastagma* (βάσταγμα), something specifically meaning "*that which is borne, a burden*" (*LS*),[16] but it is not used in the Greek Apostolic Scriptures.

What the healed man specifically carried was a *krabbatos* (κράββατος), or "*a pallet, camp bed*" (*Thayer*).[17] UBSHNT renders *krabbatos* as *mishkav* (מִשְׁכָּב), or simply "bed." While sizes of beds no doubt differed, it is doubtful that this invalid's pallet was something large and heavy. *AMG* offers the following valuable description of a *krabbatos*: "A small couch used by the poor. It denotes a simple kind of bed. . .[which] usually consisted of a padded quilt or thin mattress to be used according to the season or the condition of the owner with or without covering."[18]

With a proper understanding of *Pikku'ach Nefesh*, Yeshua did not violate the Sabbath at all by telling the healed man to pick up his pallet that was a light bed, which likely only weighed a few pounds. Yeshua did, however, no doubt "violate" the theological opinions of the group or sect of Pharisees who watched Him. Stern observes in his *Jewish New Testament Commentary*, "they could not see that the formerly crippled man's ability to carry his mat attested to God's glory."[19]

The arguments from those who do not want to keep *Shabbat* will go on and on. Many people will try to present cases that seemingly prove that Messiah Yeshua—the sinless Lamb of God

---

[15] *BDB*, 672.

[16] *LS*, 148.

[17] *Thayer*, 358.

[18] Spiros Zodhiates, ed., *Complete Word Study Dictionary: New Testament* (Chattanooga: AMG Publishers, 1993), 883.

[19] David H. Stern, *Jewish New Testament Commentary* (Clarksville, MD: Jewish New Testament Publications, 1992), 168.

and who is of one accord with His Father (cf. John 10:30)—violated the Sabbath and broke His own commandments. Sadly, these arguments are often not placed within the framework of First Century Judaism, and often relate to Christians' ignorance of the historical occurrence of Biblical events.[20]

Why do Christians assemble on Sunday?

Even though it is apparent that Messiah Yeshua kept the Sabbath and did not "violate" it, why do Christians by-and-large today assemble on Sunday? Why do they not keep the seventh-day Sabbath?

If you ask them these questions, most Christians will tell you that it is because Yeshua was resurrected from the dead on Sunday morning, and they go to church on Sunday to remember this.[21] While this was the pattern of many in the Second and Third Century Church, it was not the practice of the Jewish Apostles. The common pattern of the Apostle Paul in Acts was to always go to the local synagogue *first*, on *Shabbat*, to share the gospel with those assembled (cf. Acts 17:1). However, the historical transition from *Shabbat* to Sunday Church did take place as the emerging Church distanced itself from its Hebraic Roots and spiritual heritage in Judaism, and the Jewish Synagogue ejected and ex-communicated many of the Messianic Believers.

---

[20] D.J. Moo, who does not have a particularly high view of the Mosaic Torah for Believers today, does admit how Yeshua did not break the Sabbath:

"Certainly Jesus and his disciples violated the scribal Sabbath regulations. . .these activities [were not] a clear violation of the Mosaic Sabbath rules. . .The most that can be said is that his initiative in healing on the Sabbath, rooted in theological conviction—'it was necessary' for Jesus to heal on the Sabbath (Lk 13:16)—stretches the Sabbath commandment. But we have no evidence that Jesus ever himself violated, or approved of his disciples violating, the written Sabbath commandment" ("Law," in Joel B. Green, Scot McKnight, and I. Howard Marshall, eds., *Dictionary of Jesus and the Gospels* [Downers Grove, IL: InterVarsity, 1992], pp 454-455).

[21] While it is difficult to deny how the empty tomb was found on Sunday morning (Mark 16:2, 9; Luke 24:1; John 20:1), the earthquake that signaled Yeshua's resurrection (Matthew 28:2) occurred as the Marys approached the tomb *Opse de sabbatōn* ('Οψὲ δὲ σαββάτων) or "late on the sabbath day" (Matthew 28:1, American Standard Version). Being delayed by the earthquake, they returned in the morning to find the tomb of Yeshua vacated.

Did the early Believers meet on Sunday?

Although today's Messianics believe that the New Testament is clear that the Messiah upheld the Sabbath, there are those who tell us that His early followers did not keep *Shabbat* and instead replaced it by assembling on the first day. This is usually based on verses such as Acts 20:7, "On the first day of the week we came together to break bread" (NIV). In 1 Corinthians 16:2 Paul writes, "On the first day of every week each one of you is to put aside and save, as he may prosper, so that no collections be made when I come."

When examining these two verses, it may seem to some that the early Believers did gather on the first day of the week or Sunday. There is certainly nothing morally reprehensible about this. But even if they did assemble on Sunday, there is no indication that they *did not* likewise observe *Shabbat*. The Corinthian congregation, for example, held its meetings right next to the Corinthian synagogue (Acts 18:7-8). Sunday could have been easily set aside for the business matters of the local assembly, as opposed to being the principal day of assembling for worship, prayer, and teaching.

When placed in its correct historical and cultural context, the idea that the Believers assembling on "the first of the week" here, being what would later become the Christian Sunday, is not a complete picture. Acts 20:7, depicting the scene in Troas, is actually translated in the Complete Jewish Bible as, "On *Motza'ei Shabbat*, when we were gathered to break bread, Sha'ul addressed them. Since he was going to leave the next day, he kept talking until midnight."

Stern comments that "***Motza'ei Shabbat*** [מוצאי שבת] in Hebrew means 'departure of the Sabbath' and refers to Saturday night. . ..It would be natural for Jewish believers who had rested on *Shabbat* with the rest of the Jewish community to assemble afterwards to celebrate their common faith in Yeshua the Messiah. . ..A Saturday night meeting would continue the God-oriented spirit of *Shabbat*, rather than require the believers to shift their concern from workaday matters, as would be the case [if this were] Sunday night."[22]

The new day Biblically begins in the evening (Genesis 1:5), so the first day of the week actually begins on Saturday night. If this were speaking of Sunday night, as many believe, then technically Acts 20:7 should have read that they were meeting "on the second day of the week" as Paul, "intended to leave the next day, [but] kept on talking until midnight" (NIV). Interestingly enough, the New English Bible renders Acts 20:7 with, "On the Saturday night," recognizing the common Jewish practice.[23]

But what about 1 Corinthians 16:2: "On the first day of every week, each of you is to put something aside and store it up, as he may prosper, so that contributions need not be made when I come" (RSV)? The CJB translates this with *Motza'ei Shabbat* as well: "Every week, on *Motza'ei Shabbat*, each of you should set some money aside, according to his resources, and save it up; so that when I come I won't have to do fundraising."

1 Corinthians 16:2 has little, if nothing, to do with "Sunday Church" as is commonly observed today. At the very least, what it speaks of is people tithing their financial resources to the local assembly. Because engaging in commerce is widely prohibited on *Shabbat*, doing this when the Sabbath was over was appropriate for the First Century Messianic community, as then related business could be conducted, along with any other discussion of finances.

I would concede that if this is speaking of monetary collection for the local assembly, some of it may have occurred on a Sunday day, independent of a Saturday evening gathering. But, this does not negate the importance of *Shabbat*, nor does it annul it as some believe. For Acts 2:46 tells us that the early Believers were meeting together *kath hēmeran* (καθ' ἡμέραν) or "Every day" (NIV). There is

---

[22] David H. Stern, *Jewish New Testament Commentary* (Clarksville, MD: Jewish New Testament Publications, 1992), pp 297-298.

[23] Commentators are not fully agreed as to whether the Jewish or Roman reckoning for time is fully used by Luke in Acts.

See I. Howard Marshall, *Tyndale New Testament Commentaries: Acts* (Grand Rapids: Eerdmans, 1980), pp 325-326; Ajith Fernando, *NIV Application Commentary: Acts* (Grand Rapids: Zondervan, 1998), 530; J.C. Laansma, "Lord's Day," in Ralph P. Martin and Peter H. Davids, eds., *Dictionary of the Later New Testament & Its Developments* (Downers Grove, IL: InterVarsity, 1997), 681.

nothing wrong, Biblically, with meeting with other Believers on Sunday; **Sunday is just not the Sabbath.**

Must it be "repeated" in the New Testament?

In spite of some of the evidence seen that Messiah Yeshua did not break *Shabbat*, there will still be those who do not keep the seventh-day Sabbath. Many may deliberately dishonor the Sabbath, claiming that because there is no specific "command" in the Apostolic Scriptures (New Testament) to "do it," that they should not. Yet, there is no recorded instance in the Apostolic Scriptures of the Apostles *not* keeping the seventh-day Sabbath, or instructing the Believers *not* to keep it. In fact, the Book of Acts indicates that the Apostle Paul continued to observe the Sabbath following his conversion of faith (Acts 13:14, 42, 44; 16:13; 18:4). Furthermore, we also note that Acts 15:21 states, "For Moses from ancient generations has in every city those who preach him, since he is read in the synagogues every Sabbath," as the non-Jewish Believers were anticipated to go to Synagogue and hear the Torah and the Prophets, the only Scripture available at the time.[24]

The logic that "it's not in the New Testament" could be used to deny other important Biblical practices as well. There is no explicit command in the Apostolic Scriptures that forbids sexual relations with animals, for example. But this is a sin. This is a specific instruction given in the Torah, and we must follow it as it is for our own good (Deuteronomy 10:13).

What this ultimately comes down to is how much we want to follow the example of Yeshua. He kept the Sabbath and did not break it. He did not disobey His Father, and being one with the Father the *Shabbat* commandments are His commandments. Yeshua says, "If you keep My commandments, you will abide in My love; just as I have kept My Father's commandments and abide in His love" (John 15:10). John likewise says, "By this we know that we love the children of God, when we love God and observe His

[24] For a further discussion, consult the commentary *Acts 15 for the Practical Messianic* by J.K. McKee.

Also consult the article "Does the New Testament Annul the Biblical Appointments?" by J.K. McKee, appearing in *Torah In the Balance, Volume I.*

commandments" (1 John 5:2). Love for God should motivate us to meet with Him on *Shabbat!*

Many have said that Yeshua was only speaking of His commandments here, and would say that He is not telling His followers to observe God's commandments. But those who say that Yeshua's commandments are not God's commandments may (whether they have thought about it or not) actually telling us that Yeshua is not God—and thus not a Divine Savior. Obviously, we cannot accept this. If we want to follow the Messiah's example then we will endeavor to obey the Torah and keep *Shabbat* as He did.

Many will say, though, that by the Second and Third Centuries Christians were observing Sunday and not the Sabbath. These people will use quotations from Church history to prove that it was their custom to observe Sunday, and so should we. Yet, there is no Biblical basis for this change. As George Eldon Ladd astutely comments, "Let it be at once emphasized that we [should not turn] to the church fathers to find authority...The one authority is the Word of God, and we are not confined in the straight-jacket of tradition."[25] While these comments were delivered in regard to the pre- versus post-tribulation rapture controversy, Ladd is correct. Regardless of what the Church Fathers taught, we must seek our answers from the Scriptures and the actual writings of the Apostles first—because those who came later might have been wrong on this issue.

Notably, the Apostle Paul wrote that "the secret power of lawlessness is already at work" (2 Thessalonians 2:7, NIV). Indeed, if this lawlessness or denial of God's Torah was at work at the time when he wrote this in the mid-First Century, then is it possible that by the end of the First Century *Shabbat* was not being kept by many Believers? By the Second to Third Centuries, Church writings indeed prove that Sunday took *Shabbat*'s place, by-and-large.[26] But simply because these Church writings say that most Believers in the Second and Third Centuries did not keep the seventh-day

---

[25] George Eldon Ladd, *The Blessed Hope* (Grand Rapids: Eerdmans, 1956), 19.

[26] For a compilation of quotes among Second-Third Century C.E. Church leaders regarding the Sabbath, consult "Sabbath," in David W. Bercot, ed., *A Dictionary of Early Christian Beliefs* (Peabody, MA: Hendrickson, 1998), pp 571-572; "Lord's Day," in Ibid., pp 405-407.

Sabbath, does not make it right. Our job is to return to the faith of the original Believers in Messiah Yeshua who kept *Shabbat*. We remember the Sabbath not just as an institution from Creation, but because Yeshua and His Apostles remembered it.

Is Sunday truly a "Sabbath"?

Others believe that the New Testament "changed" the Sabbath to Sunday. Many of these Christians honestly strive to observe a "Sunday Sabbath" and dedicate the entire day to God as *Shabbat* is supposed to be. Much of Reformation and post-Reformation history is marked by the examples of those who faithfully kept a Sunday Sabbath. However, due to the fast pace of our Western culture *today* in the Twenty-First Century, most who try to observe a "Sunday Sabbath" are not able to dedicate a day completely unto the Lord as did their forbearers—more than anything else because this is not encouraged in the contemporary Christian Church.

I would ask you to consider some of the reasons why God wanted His people to rest:

"Then Moses assembled all the congregation of the sons of Israel, and said to them, 'These are the things that the LORD has commanded *you* to do: For six days work may be done, but on the seventh day you shall have a holy *day*, a sabbath of complete rest to the LORD; whoever does any work on it shall be put to death" (Exodus 35:1-2).

The Israelites who were constructing the Tabernacle, as well as working in their daily tasks in the camp during the wilderness trek, were working long and hard hours under difficult conditions. The Lord told them to take a day of complete and total rest—what the Hebrew calls a *qodesh Shabbat shabbaton l'ADONAI* (שַׁבַּת שַׁבָּתוֹן לַיהוָה קֹדֶשׁ), or a holy Sabbath day of rest to the Lord.

While we can understand why this command was given to the Ancient Israelites back then, because they were working under hard circumstances, some do not believe that God would ask us today to take the seventh day and consecrate it entirely unto Him. After all, are there not things to do on Saturday? Saturday is the day when all the stores are open late and you can get the best deals at the mall. New movies have opened at the theater. All the good ball games are on and you can sit in front of the television and tune into the world. Yet, when we really do think about the fast pace and demands of modern life, remembering the Sabbath probably has more relevance ***now*** than it did for the ancients!

Contrary to what many may think, God indeed has the right to tell us today in the Twenty-First Century that we should consecrate a day entirely unto Him. He wants to commune with His people, and by resting in Him we not only rejuvenate our bodies—but we also rejuvenate our spirits by delving deeper and deeper into His Word—and remove ourselves from outside influences. While none of us can keep the Sabbath command perfectly, we do have the blood covering of Yeshua, and if we follow His example we should strive to honor the Sabbath to the best of our ability. He gave it all up for us by coming down to Earth from the right hand of the Father. *What is one day out of our week specially devoted to Him?*

But some will say that they observe the Sabbath. They will say that they go to church on Sunday. But Sunday is not the seventh day, and these Christians' Sabbath is usually between *only one and two hours long*. After their church services, many Christians go out to eat or go shopping, not taking a day of complete and total rest. Their "substitute Sabbath" is really no Sabbath at all, and many may be found wanting by the Lord of the Sabbath.[27]

Others will say that they "rest in Christ." After all, as Hebrews 4:9-10 says, "There remains therefore a Sabbath rest for the people of God. For the one who has entered His rest has himself also rested from his works, as God did from His." But is "Sabbath rest" what the text fully conveys? The Sabbath is certainly about rest, but the Greek *sabbatismos* (σαββατισμός) means "***sabbath rest, sabbath observance***" (*BDAG*).[28] As the Complete Jewish Bible renders Hebrews 4:9: "So there remains a *Shabbat*-keeping for God's people." In defense of this translation, Stern states, "Greek *sabbatismos*, [is] used only here in the New Testament. In the Septuagint, the related Greek word '*sabbatizein*' [sic][29] was coined to translate the Hebrew verb *shabat* [שָׁבַת] when it means 'to observe *Shabbat*.' The usual translation, 'There remains a Sabbath

[27] Matthew 12:8; Mark 2:28; Luke 6:5.

[28] *BDAG*, 909.

[29] Grk. LXX: *esabbatisen* (ἐσαββάτισεν), aorist active third person singular, used Exodus 16:30; *sabbatizein* (σαββατίζειν), present active infinitive, is used in 2 Maccabees 6:6.

rest,' minimizes the observance aspect and makes the role of God's people entirely passive."[30]

As Believers, it is important that we understand that we have an *active faith*—not a passive faith where we can "spiritually rest" in the Messiah, but not keep the Sabbath or any kind of physical rest. While we must remember and focus on Yeshua on *Shabbat*, we cannot dispense with it and say that we are keeping it "in Christ," as do many who really do not keep it, or perhaps make any effort to keep it. Remembering the Sabbath *physically* enables us to understand the greater spiritual realities that *Shabbat* typifies.

Dedicating one day out of our week entirely to our Heavenly Father is not difficult, and while you may get some criticism for it from others—the rewards are well worth it! Pleasing God is much better than pleasing others.

Is Sunday "the Lord's Day"?

Now that we have discussed the Biblical importance of *Shabbat*, and some of the reasons why we as Believers in Messiah Yeshua should keep it, we are now in an appropriate position to discuss that "the Lord's Day" is not Sunday.

The Apostle John says in Revelation 1:10 that "I was in the Spirit on the Lord's day, and I heard behind me a loud voice like *the sound* of a trumpet." Many prophecy commentators, both pre- and post-tribulational, believe that this is speaking of Sunday. Ladd states that "It is. . .likely that [what] we see here [is] the emerging language referring to the Lord's day as the Christians' distinctive day of religious devotion. . .The emergence of Sunday observance in place of the Jewish Sabbath was a gradual historical process, and here we have the beginning of that process."[31] Supposedly, when the Apostle John was shown his vision of the end-times, he was shown it on Sunday.

Many Messianics believe that "the Lord's Day" mentioned in Revelation 1:10 is not Sunday, but rather the Day of the LORD, the end-time period of God's judgment on the world and His vindication of the righteous. This would have more relevance in relation to the

---

[30] Stern, *Jewish New Testament Commentary*, 673.

[31] George Eldon Ladd, *A Commentary on the Revelation of John* (Grand Rapids: Eerdmans, 1972), 31.

subject matter of Yeshua's revelation to the Apostle John, because if the Lord's Day is Sunday, it may just be a minor detail that is relatively unimportant given the wider scope and message of the book he writes.[32] But if it is in reference to the Day of the LORD, then it is very important that we pay attention.

Notably, Revelation 1:10 in the Complete Jewish Bible is rendered with, "I came to be, in the Spirit, on **the Day of the Lord**; and I heard behind me a loud voice, like a trumpet." Justifying this, Stern comments, "Yochanan [John] is reporting the unique experience of having seen God's final Judgment."[33]

Some say that "the Lord's Day" of Revelation 1:10 cannot be "the Day of the Lord," because of the unique Greek used in this passage. In the Septuagint, the "Day of the LORD" representative of *Yom ADONAI* (יוֹם יְהוָה), is usually represented as *hēmera (tou) Kuriou* (ἡμέρα "τοῦ κυρίου). But what appears in Revelation 1:10 is *tē Kuriakē hēmera* (τῇ κυριακῇ ἡμέρᾳ), literally "the Lord's Day." Due to this odd Greek, it is often said that "the Lord's Day" cannot be the Day of the LORD.[34]

The Greek adjective *kuriakos* (κυριακός), translated as "Lord's," "**pert. to belonging to the Lord, *the Lord's***" (*BDAG*).[35] The only other place *kuriakos* is used in the Apostolic Scriptures is in 1 Corinthians 11:20: "Therefore when you meet together, it is not to eat the Lord's Supper [*Kuriakon deipnon*, κυριακὸν δεῖπνον]." Stern states that it "speaks of 'a meal of the Lord,' that is, pertaining to the Lord. . .a meal eaten in a manner worthy of Yeshua or of God."[36]

While I believe that "the Lord's Day" is most likely speaking of the Day of the LORD, there is a second alternative to Sunday Church that we can consider. The Book of Revelation is "A revelation [or revealing] of Yeshua the Messiah" (Revelation 1:1), and it is a time

---

[32] Consult the entry for Revelation 1:10 in the *Messianic Sabbath Helper*.

[33] Stern, *Jewish New Testament Commentary*, 791.

[34] While advocating that Sunday Church is in view in Revelation 1:10, J.C. Laansma does still acknowledge, though, "There are many ways of referring to the Day of the Lord, and Revelation 1:10 may be one more" ("Lord's Day," in *Dictionary of the Later New Testament and Its Developments*, 682). He at least recognizes this as a possibility, not far fetched given the themes of Revelation.

[35] *BDAG*, 576.

[36] Stern, *Jewish New Testament Commentary*, 791.

period that pertains to the Lord and to His work on behalf of His people (cf. Revelation 6:10). As Revelation speaks of the end-times, it is perhaps fitting to understand "the Lord's Day" as a time that has special meaning for the Messiah and His followers. It could be speaking of the Holy Spirit being poured out upon God's people and Yeshua revealing Himself to the world as the King of Kings and Lord of Lords in a manner not ever experienced before (cf. Matthew 24:21).

"The Lord's Day" may be speaking of a future period of time that in addition to "the Day of the LORD," concerns Believers being involved in the Lord's service in a way that they have never experienced before. The Tribulation saints are notably those "who keep the commandments of God and hold to the testimony of Yeshua" (Revelation 12:17). Is it possible that if "the Lord's Day" is a time during the Tribulation where He is revealed to His people like never before—and that this kind of revealing is contingent on them obeying His commandments in the Torah—that *Shabbat*, being a distinguishing sign, is somehow involved? The Millennium that will follow *is to some degree* typified as being a kind of Sabbath rest.

So is Sunday "the Lord's Day?" In the sense that God is the Master of Creation and all things are His—including time and *all* the days of the week—yes. But in the sense that Sunday is now "the Sabbath" or a "special day" formed in New Testament times, ***no***. The reference to "the Lord's Day" in Revelation 1:10 is either speaking of the end-time Day of the LORD, or a time unlike any other where Messiah Yeshua is revealed to His followers and the world.

Christians Have Missed Out on a Blessing

The change from the Sabbath to Sunday does not have a firm foundation when one sticks to Scripture. If we wish to follow our Lord's example, then we will keep the Sabbath and concentrate on Him and His work for us for an entire day. As it might be our sad observation, though, many Christians will continue to miss out on the blessings of *Shabbat*, living lives where they are physically burned out and desiring rest, but not knowing where to find it. But it has been our **sadder observation** that some Messianics will berate these Christians, saying that they go to church on "SUNday" and are not true Believers, and are in actuality worshipping the sun god rather than the Holy One of Israel. This is because Sunday was the preferred day of worship in the Roman Empire and was the venerable day of the Sun.

Irvin and Sunquist remark in *History of the World Christian Movement* that when Constantine made Christianity a legal religion within the Roman Empire in the Fourth Century C.E., he "spoke of being a servant of God. Yet publicly he continued to mix Christian piety with devotion to the high solar deity, the Invincible Sun, which had become popular with the emperors of the previous century. When he declared in 321 that Sunday be set apart as a special day of worship, it is not clear whether it was the Invincible Sun or Jesus Christ whom he intended to honor."[37]

Many people are unaware of history, and criticizing Christians of worshipping the sun god **is completely unfounded to those in ignorance**—especially as we should be worshipping and serving God *every day* and it is certainly not wrong to worship Him on Sunday, even though it is not the Biblical Sabbath. It is not becoming of the example of Yeshua to treat Christians who go to church on Sunday and do not keep *Shabbat* as total pagans, especially since those usually criticizing surely did not consider *themselves* as pagans when they went to church on Sunday. Criticizing without fairness or mercy will cause more problems. We need to be part of the solution, demonstrating the blessings of *Shabbat* to our Christian brethren.

I do not believe that Christians who go to church on Sunday are worshipping another God or a different Savior. Only God Himself can determine the true heart intent of Christians who are observing Sunday, and likewise that of any Messianics who harshly criticize them. However, keeping the Sabbath and dedicating an entire day to God, as opposed to a few hours on Sunday, has its added blessings as it is the day that He set-apart and sanctified. It is the time when we can rest from all our labors, rejuvenate ourselves, fellowship with other Believers, study the Word, and look forward to the greater rest to come in the eschaton.

---

[37] Dale T. Irvin and Scott W. Sunquist, *History of the World Christian Movement*, Vol. 1 (Maryknoll, NY: Orbis Books, 2001), 162.

But just as some Messianics vehemently criticize those who do not keep the Sabbath, there are certainly those Christians who do the same in reverse. Many of these will say that by not going to church on Sunday, we are denying the resurrection of Yeshua whose empty tomb was found on this day. This *is not the case*, at least for our ministry.[38] On the contrary, if we truly want to *live* like Yeshua, then we will honor the Sabbath as He did—and it will be a blessing for us.

We do recognize that there are true Believers who are presently not convicted that they should honor the Sabbath. Many of these people know the Lord, but are still maturing in their walk. *But they do not speak against those who keep the seventh-day Sabbath.* We hope that if you belong to this category, and you do not totally understand the Sabbath, that you will at least give Messianics like us the freedom to follow Yeshua's example. At the very least, may your position be that of the late Walter Martin:

"I believe Seventh-Day Adventists, Seventh-day Baptists and Sabbatarians of other religious groups have the right to worship on the seventh day in the liberty wherein Christ has made us free. It is wrong and un-Christian to discriminate against Sabbatarians merely because they 'esteem' the Sabbath above the first day of the week, or Lord's Day. I suggest it is no more legalistic for them to observe the seventh day out of conviction than it is for the Christian Church to observe the first day. It is a matter of liberty and conscience."[39]

Martin, while believing that "the Lord's Day" should be observed instead of *Shabbat*, was fair and loving to those who kept the seventh-day Sabbath, recognizing it as a Biblical ordinance that *should not be spoken against*. He believed it was wrong to criticize and berate those who observed *Shabbat*, although he himself did not. He certainly did not consider those who honored the seventh-day Sabbath to be "unsaved." He did not consider it a salvation issue, but rather one of personal choice.

Messianics who want to encourage positive change among all Believers, and impact Christians intrigued by the Hebraic Roots of their faith, must do the same to a certain degree. We cannot

---

[38] Consult the relevant sections of the *Messianic Spring Holiday Helper*.

[39] Walter R. Martin, *The Kingdom of the Cults* (Minneapolis: Bethany House Publishers, 1985), 470.

discriminate against those who do not keep the Sabbath, but we must show them the blessings and rest they have missed out on by not fully living the life of the Messiah who kept *Shabbat*. As we follow the Sabbath-keeping of our Lord, we must also follow His example and love those who do not presently keep *Shabbat*. We must emulate Messiah Yeshua who observed the seventh-day Sabbath, and by emulating Him hopefully others will emulate us. May they see the blessings of *Shabbat* present in our lives, and want them as well!

We believe that when you devote an entire day to God and keep *Shabbat*, many do find that they will not want to go back to the limitations of Sunday Church. *You will be experiencing **more** of God, and not less!* We believe that you will find that by keeping the Sabbath with the empowerment of the Holy Spirit, that the rewards of doing things the way He intended will truly be great—and you will want to tell others about it. It will be a way to live out Yeshua's word, "Let your light shine before men in such a way that they may see your good works, and glorify your Father who is in heaven" (Matthew 5:16). Today's Messianic Believers, who keep the seventh-day Sabbath/*Shabbat*, will certainly be in a much better place to testify to Jewish people who are inquiring of Israel's Messiah, than those who think that Israel's Messiah abolished it.

How Did We Lose the Sabbath?

When many of us think about some of the most significant theological debates of the past three or five decades, we are probably immediately drawn into thinking about conservatives and liberals sparring over the reliability of the Holy Scriptures, creationists and evolutionists fighting about the origins of humankind, Scripturalists and cultists warring over the Divinity of Yeshua, and most recently the controversy that has been rising up over homosexuality and gay marriage.[1] How many of us are consciously aware that there has been a debate ensuing among evangelical Christians, and various others, for over three decades surrounding **the Sabbath**? Books written in favor of continuance of the seventh-day Sabbath have been written, along with cross-examinations and refutations.[2]

Certainly, the controversy of the seventh-day Sabbath, and the widespread Christian observance of Sunday Church, might seem a

---

[1] For a review of all of these issues, at least in part, consult *Confronting Critical Issues: An Analysis of Subjects that Affects the Growth and Stability of the Emerging Messianic Movement* by J.K. McKee.

[2] Two books that have widely framed the debate are Samuele Bacchiocchi, *From Sabbath to Sunday* (Rome: Pontifical Gregorian University Press, 1977), defending the validity of the seventh-day Sabbath from a Seventh-Day Adventist perspective, and D.A. Carson, ed., *From Sabbath to Lord's Day* (Eugene, OR: Wipf and Stock, 1999 [1982 actual publication]), cross-examining Bacchiocchi and defending Sunday as "the Lord's Day" from a broadly evangelical viewpoint.

A more recent analysis from a Seventh-Day Adventist standpoint is Sigve K. Tonstad, *The Lost Meaning of the Seventh Day* (Berrien Springs, MI: Andrews University Press, 2009). More general is Christopher John Donato, ed., *Perspectives on the Sabbath: Four Views* (Nashville: B&H Academic, 2011).

bit mundane to various people. At the same time, if the widespread practice of Sunday church is in error to some degree—than even with many other evangelical Christian doctrines widely correct—a significant opportunity for physical rest and spiritual refreshment for God's people has been too often lost, or even outright forfeited. Further to be realized is how a dismissal of the seventh-day Sabbath, by many in the emerging Christian Church of the Second and Third Centuries, would be shown to be the result of an unwarranted anti-Semitism and purposeful distance from the Jewish Synagogue and Hebraic origins of Messiah faith.

It is frequently heard from people throughout much of today's Messianic movement, and most especially the more independent Hebrew/Hebraic Roots movement, that the Sabbath was changed by the Emperor Constantine, so that he could continue some form of sun/solar worship via the guise of Christianity and syncretism. There is little doubting the fact that the Emperor Constantine, in the Fourth Century, did enact various laws by which the first day of the week was legislated as an important time for a newly legal Christian religion. However, when one delves more into the debate over the continued validity of the seventh-day Sabbath or *Shabbat* (שַׁבָּת), you quickly have to evaluate not just various religious-political motivations of the period of Constantine and soon thereafter—you have to also deal with theological motivations of the late First and early Second Centuries, *and* various passages of the Apostolic Scriptures or New Testament (i.e., Acts 20:7; 1 Corinthians 16:2).[3] To just say that "Constantine changed it" would be an overly-simplistic view. In fact, the 2011 volume *Perspectives on the Sabbath: Four Views*, reflects that there are, and have been, multiple perspectives present on the Sabbath issue throughout a wide scope of Christian history, including:

1. the continuity of the seventh-day Sabbath
2. Sunday as the new Christian Sabbath
3. the seventh-day Sabbath as a temporary prescription for Ancient Israel

---

[3] Much of the debate, that has been witnessed over the validity of the seventh-day Sabbath, has actually more to do about the validity of the Torah or Law of Moses for Messiah followers, than the Sabbath issue itself. This has been thoroughly addressed in *The New Testament Validates Torah* by J.K. McKee, as well as throughout the *Messianic Torah Helper* by Messianic Apologetics.

4. Sabbath now representative of a spiritual rest in the Messiah for Believers

The latter two views listed would argue for a total abolition of the Fourth Commandment (Exodus 20:8; Deuteronomy 5:12), whereas the first two views would strongly agree with the concept of a Sabbath-principle, although they disagree on the day of the week to observe it. That the issue of the seventh-day Sabbath, and its continuance for God's people, has been a debate present in various degrees, does not go unnoticed by various theological resources. A general Bible dictionary like *EDB* closes its entry on the Sabbath with the following observations,

"The Scriptures have left some questions concerning the sabbath unanswered. Not only are some particulars of sabbath regulations unclear, but the fundamental question of whether or not the sabbath was completely fulfilled by Christ's first coming has plagued Christianity and is still a debated topic. The choice of the day also presents a point of disagreement, with some groups continuing to adhere to the Jewish practice of a Saturday sabbath."[4]

Today's Messianic movement—even with its diversity, and with a wide degree of applications over *Shabbat* observance—widely does believe that the seventh-day Sabbath remains an instruction to be observed in perpetuity. It is widely recognized that some changes were instituted by Christians of the Second Century for sure, with many abandoning the seventh-day Sabbath, for some kind of activity on Sunday. It is also widely recognized that the Emperor Constantine, and later Church councils, made observance of Sunday as a religious day, a legal requirement, with the seventh-day Sabbath as something to be dismissed. Some gaps do have to be filled, though, in terms of specific Christian voices deriding the seventh-day Sabbath.

One will get various admissions of anti-Semitism, and certainly anti-Sabbatarianism, on the part of many Second-Fourth Century Church leaders, by today's contemporary Christian theologians and historians. Today's Messianic community has to fairly sort through some of this history, recognizing the loss of the seventh-day

---

[4] Ann Coble, "Sabbath," in David Noel Freedman, ed., *Eerdmans Dictionary of the Bible* (Grand Rapids: Eerdmans, 2000), 1146.

Sabbath as a great error which needs to be corrected for sure—but corrected with a proper scope of the facts, tempered by a recognition of how, in the words of Skip MacCarty,

"The Sabbath has helped God seem more real to us and nurtured our relationship with Him....[we should] not take the position that all Christians who presently worship on a different day do not love Jesus or have the assurance of salvation."[5]

Indeed, today's Messianic movement is being strategically placed to be a representation of what is coming in the Messianic era, when worldwide Sabbath observance is going to be unambiguously universal for all humanity, enforced from Zion by the Messiah Himself (Isaiah 66:23). As we examine some of the mistakes made in past history, we have to also recognize that we cannot do anything to change the past—but we can do everything to accelerate the future. We are a unique and special faith community, taking the strengths of Judaism and Christianity, and moving forward with them. A dismissal of the seventh-day Sabbath on the part of many throughout Christian history, is being rectified in our day by the Messianic community for sure—as we are consciously recapturing the faith practices of the early Believers in Israel's Messiah.

Sabbath Among the First Century Believers

When reviewing a broad spectrum of theological resources today, there is frequent uniformity of recognition in how Yeshua the Messiah (Jesus Christ) and His Disciples all observed the seventh-day Sabbath or *Shabbat*. There is disagreement as to how much or how little Yeshua observed various traditional and customary applications of "work" imposed by the Pharisaical leaders, but few would say that Yeshua's presumed violations of the Sabbath were outright acts of disobedience of Mosaic commandments. Some might say that Yeshua's violation of some of the strict interpretations of Sabbath instruction was with the intention that the Sabbath be abrogated subsequent to His resurrection. More will be prone to say that Yeshua followed a more liberal interpretation of the permissive applications of

[5] Skip MacCarty, "The Seventh-Day Sabbath," in *Perspectives on the Sabbath: Four Views*, 9.

Sabbath instructions, whereby people could be healed of their infirmities, and care could indeed be expelled, to facilitate human wholeness. Willard M. Swartley offers the following summary from the *Dictionary of Scripture and Ethics:*

> "Jesus and his disciples observed the Sabbath (Mark 1:21; Luke 4:16; 23:56b), although Jesus tangled with the Pharisees over Sabbath laws...Jesus healed on the Sabbath, allowing physical exertion on that day: taking up one's mat and walking (John 5:2-12), plucking grain (Mark 2:23-28), and washing in a pool (John 9:1-12). Jesus' Sabbath actions spiraled into mortal conflict with the religious leaders.
>
> "Jesus explains his Sabbath practices as life-affirming: 'The sabbath was made for humankind; and not humankind for the sabbath,' and therefore 'the Son of Man is lord even of the sabbath' (Mark 2:27-28). In speech and action Jesus fulfills the Sabbath, bringing rest to the weary (Matt. 11:28-29) with human liberation."[6]

The narrative of Luke 4:16 details, "as was His custom, He entered the synagogue on the Sabbath," indicating how "As he always did on the Sabbath, he went to the meeting place" (The Message). Yeshua the Messiah not only kept the seventh-day Sabbath, but going to synagogue on the Sabbath was something that He was accustomed to doing.

Following the Messiah's ascension into Heaven, the record of the Book of Acts indicates that for certain, as the good news spread into the Mediterranean basin, figures like the Apostle Paul would go to Diaspora Jewish synagogues on the Sabbath, and use the Sabbath as an opportunity to testify to his fellow Jews, as well as Greek and Roman God-fearers. Most of the assemblies, to which Paul would write letters, got their start because of some kind of gospel declaration by Paul at a Diaspora synagogue on *Shabbat*. In the case of Philippi (Acts 16:11-40), the Sabbath fellowship that met outside the city was seemingly transformed into a community of Messiah followers. In the case of Corinth (Acts 18:1-18), though, the Messiah followers were ejected from the synagogue, yet they met at a home right next to the synagogue. From the narrative of

---

[6] Willard M. Swartley, "Sabbath," in Joel B. Green, ed. et. al., *Dictionary of Scripture and Ethics* (Grand Rapids: Baker Academic, 2011), 695.

the Book of Acts, aside from a departure fellowship gathering for Paul at Troas "on the first of the week"[7] (Acts 20:7, PME), there is no quantitative abandonment of the Sabbath.

The Jewish Believers for certain continued to observe *Shabbat*, often in connection with the local Jewish community. The non-Jewish Believers, being participants in Tanach prophecy as anticipated by James the Just (Acts 15:15), when following the Apostolic decree (Acts 15:19-21, 29), would find themselves cut off from their old, pagan spheres of religious and social influence—and find their new sphere of religious and social influence to be one where Moses' Teaching was being taught every Sabbath (Acts 15:21). *ABD* further addresses how within the Book of Acts,

> "Aside from two casual references to the sabbath (Acts 1:12; 15:21), the sabbath is mentioned in connection with the establishment of churches in Pisidian Antioch (13:13-52), Philippi (16:11-15), Thessalonica (17:1-9), and Corinth (18:1-4). The Western text includes Ephesus (18:19). Paul, as Jesus before him, went to the synagogue on sabbath 'as his custom was' (Acts 17:2; cf. 24:14; 28:17). There is silence on the subject of sabbath abolition at the Jerusalem Conference (15:1-29). There is also no evidence for the abrogation of the sabbath after the Jerusalem Council in the apostolic age or by apostolic authority in the early church...Early Jewish and non-Jewish Christians continued to worship on the seventh day as far as the evidence of the book of Acts is concerned.
>
> "The single reference to 'the first day of the week' in Acts 20:7-12, when Christian believers broke bread in a farewell meeting at the imminent departure of Paul is debated in its meaning. Some scholars suggest that Roman reckoning is used so that 'the first day of the week' means Sunday night...and other scholars suggest that Jewish reckoning is used and in that case it means Saturday night...This passage hardly supports Sunday-keeping on the part of the apostolic church, since this was an occasional farewell meeting lasting till after

---

[7] Grk. *En de tē mia tōn sabbatōn* ('Εν δὲ τῇ μιᾷ τῶν σαββάτων); debates as to "on the first of the week" really represent are seen in the NEB/REB extrapolation "On the Saturday night" (also Phillips New Testament with, "On the Saturday"); the CJB having "On *Motza'ei-Shabbat*"; The Message has in contrast, "We met on Sunday to worship."

midnight (v 7) and the breaking of bread is hardly the Lord's Supper."[8]

Judaism was a legal and protected religion in the Roman Empire, and the Messiah followers by virtue of association with the Jewish Synagogue, were a legally protected Jewish sect. Observance of the weekly Sabbath was a significant hallmark of Jewish practice (Josephus *Life* 279; t.*Shabbat* 1:13), known to the Romans for sure (Suetonius *Tiberius* 32.2; Tacitus *Histories* 5.4). While First Century Jewish Believers in Yeshua, aside from some degree of ostracism that they may had experienced for their Messiah faith, would have continued to observe *Shabbat* as they had widely known it—the issue of Sabbath observance for the non-Jewish Greek and Roman Believers is a little more complicated.

Many of the first non-Jewish Believers to recognize Israel's Messiah were taken from among the God-fearers, who are often regarded as Greeks and Romans who had recognized Israel's God, and had taken on various levels of Torah observance, notably including the seventh-day Sabbath and appointed times. They often, for various reasons, stopped short of being circumcised as full-fledged proselytes, such as Cornelius being a Roman centurion (Acts 10:2) and circumcision possibly being an issue of treason. Non-Jewish Believers who were God-fearers, with many integrated within the Jewish community already, would have continued to observe the Sabbath. Non-Jewish Believers who had been idolaters, upon recognizing Israel's Messiah, are not witnessed in the Apostolic Scriptures to have had the Sabbath mandated upon them, which leads interpreters to various conclusions.

Many Christian readers of the Pauline letters think that the Apostle abrogated or abolished the seventh-day Sabbath for all Believers, Jewish and non-Jewish alike, per some traditional interpretations of: Romans 14:5-6; Galatians 4:9-10; and Colossians 2:16-17.[9] Some, such as this writer, are not convinced that these

---

[8] Gerhard F. Hasel, "Sabbath," in David Noel Freedman, ed., *Anchor Bible Dictionary*, 6 vols. (New York: Doubleday, 1992), 5:855.

[9] Consult the article "Does the New Testament Annul the Biblical Appointments?", appearing in *Torah In the Balance, Volume I* by J.K. McKee.

passages abolish the seventh-day Sabbath, and have some more particularized circumstances to be considered for their original audiences, such as the Romans 14 "days" actually being optional days of fasting, and the Galatian and Colossian situations involving an influence of paganism upon Biblical practice. Still, even if these passages are not interpreted as relating to an abrogation of *Shabbat*, what were the non-Jewish Believers to do? If they recognized Israel's God and Messiah, they would be attached to a Jewish community that rested on the seventh-day. The salvation of the non-Jewish Believers was a part of the fulfillment of Tanach prophecy, which would involve the eventual, full emergence of the Messianic Age when Sabbath observance is to be worldwide (Isaiah 66:23).

One perspective, as argued by Craig S. Keener in his commentary on Romans, is that "Paul was simply pragmatic: unless they belonged to the ethnic enclave of Israel, Gentile slaves and workers normally could not observe the Sabbath fully, and Paul did not require this ideal of those who could not observe it."[10] More poignantly, it should be thought that while Sabbath observance in the Torah was an egalitarian statute, for "*in it* you shall not do any work, you or your son or your daughter, your male or your female servant or your cattle or your sojourner who stays with you" (Exodus 20:10), rather than imposing this on people in a manner akin to ordering the non-Jews to observe the Torah for salvation (Acts 15:1, 5)—James the Just recognized how the expectations of Tanach prophecy involving the nations were to occur naturally (cf. Acts 15:15). The interjection that many of the non-Jewish Believers—who undoubtedly came from the lower and slave classes (cf. 1 Corinthians 1:26)—would have found it readily difficult to observe the Sabbath, given their widespread social and economic status, cannot be ignored. For many, choosing to identify with Israel's God—rather than the gods of one's employer, patron, or owner—would have proven difficult enough.

Lengthy analyses of Romans 14; Galatians 4:9-11; and Colossians 2:16-23 are available in the **Sabbath and Rest in the Apostolic Scriptures** section of the *Messianic Sabbath Helper*.

[10] Craig S. Keener, *New Covenant Commentary Series: Romans* (Eugene, OR: Cascade Books, 2009), pp 164-165.

Those who were rich and wealthy, although few in number, could take off a Sabbath. But, to what degree would those who were poor or slaves be able to do so? If they all of a sudden started taking the seventh-day off, how many would find themselves homeless and destitute, beaten, or starved? Many were able to keep the Sabbath, and then others kept it as much as their circumstances permitted them.

Avoiding "things sacrificed to idols and from blood and from things strangled and from fornication" (Acts 15:29) was the only prescription to the new, non-Jewish Believers to be regarded as a "burden" (Acts 15:28). Rather than forcing people to do things, the Apostolic intention was much more focused on the work of the Holy Spirit in following God's Torah (cf. Romans 8:4)—which is true of both non-Jewish *and* Jewish Believers alike. Israel's Messiah took the penalties of Sabbath observance upon Himself at the tree (cf. Colossians 2:14); the promised universal Sabbath would arrive as the future world to come steadily made an influence on the present evil world. When given the choice of forcing or obligating people to do things, or letting God's plan naturally take shape at the direction and guidance of His Spirit—the latter is the only optimal choice.

Dismissal of the Seventh-Day Sabbath in Emerging Christianity

Rhetoric that is commonly witnessed throughout the independent Hebrew/Hebraic Roots movement, but has also been popularized through many, but not all members, of the Seventh-Day Adventist Church, has been the supposition that the Roman Emperor Constantine changed the Sabbath to Sunday, in the Fourth Century C.E., as a means for him to continue with his solar/sun worship. For many Protestant Christians, the issue of Christian activities on Sunday does not so much concern the activities of Constantine in the Fourth Century C.E., as much as it concerns the activities of Christians in the late First and early Second Centuries C.E., with the emergence of commemorating "the Lord's Day" on the first day of the week or Sunday. In the *Dictionary of Theological Terms*, reflecting a highly conservative Presbyterian perspective, it is asserted,

"We frequently hear the Seventh Day Adventist charge that Constantine changed the day for sabbath observance from Saturday to Sunday. This is untrue. The early church very clearly observed the first day of the week as its day for public worship (Acts 20:7; 1 Cor. 16:2). Just why Christians should have met on the first day of the week has never been satisfactorily answered by upholders of the seventh-day sabbath. Their practice is a mystery to us unless we recognize that it had apostolic sanction."[11]

The view of many, based on some traditional approaches to various New Testament passages indicating some kind of assemblage on the first day, is that a transition toward Sunday or "the Lord's Day" is one that occurred organically in the First Century *ekklēsia*, and then by the Second Century was the major practice of the emerging Christian Church, as witnessed in the works of Second to Third Century Christian leaders. This is the view reflected in a variety of easily accessible Bible dictionaries and encyclopedias. *NIDB* draws the conclusion,

"The early Christians, most of whom were Jews, kept the seventh day as a Sabbath, but since the resurrection of their Lord was the most blessed day in their lives, they began very early to meet for worship on the first day of the week (Acts 2:1) and designated it as the Lord's Day. Paul directed the Corinthian Christians to bring their weekly offering to the charities of the church on the first day of the week (1 Cor 16:1-2). As the split between Jews and Christians widened, the Christians came gradually to meet for worship only on the Lord's Day and gave up the observance of the seventh day."[12]

Noting traditional approaches to passages such as Colossians 2:16; Romans 14:5; Galatians 4:10; Acts 20:7; 1 Corinthians 16:2; and Revelation 1:10, *ISBE* more cautiously directs how replacement of the seventh-day Sabbath with Sunday or "Lord's Day" assemblages were not definite until the Second Century C.E.:

"Even the combined testimony of these texts...does not demonstrate conclusively that sabbath observance had been widely

---

[11] "Sabbath," in Alan Cairns, *Dictionary of Theological Terms* (Greenville, SC: Ambassador Emerald International, 2002), 392.

[12] Steven Barabas, "Sabbath," in Merrill C. Tenney, ed., *The New International Dictionary of the Bible* (Grand Rapids: Zondervan, 1987), 877.

replaced by observance of the Lord's Day by the end of the 1st century...They also suggest the probability that Sunday observance has its roots in the NT, although conclusive evidence for widespread Sunday observance is not found until the 2nd century."[13]

Today's Messianic community will and does have some alternative approaches to "first of the week" (Acts 20:7; 1 Corinthians 16:2) likely being informal gatherings of Believers as *Shabbat* was closing on Saturday evening, and *tē Kuriakē hēmera* (τῇ κυριακῇ ἡμέρᾳ) associated more with "the Day of the Lord" (Revelation 1:10, CJB/TLV)[14] per the end-time themes of the Book of Revelation. Still, it is an historical fact that by the Second Century, Sunday assemblages designated as "the Lord's Day" were occurring in the emerging Christian Church. Some see the roots of this as being authorized by the Apostles. Others would see the roots of this as being a misinterpretation of the writings of the Apostles, with the "first of the week" being approached from a reckoning of Roman time and not a reckoning of Jewish time. Along with this would be a misevaluation of the time when Yeshua was actually resurrected from the dead, with *Opse de sabbatōn* ('Οψὲ δὲ σαββάτων) in Matthew 28:1 being better understood as "Now late on the sabbath day" (American Standard Version), the twilight of Saturday, with the empty tomb of the Messiah subsequently found on Sunday morning.[15] Most of all, when consulting some early Christian writings about Sunday as "the Lord's Day" having apparently superseded the seventh-day Sabbath, Messianic people cannot dismiss how a tenor of either covert or overt anti-Semitism is blatantly present.

It is to be recognized how a major factor of transition, from a seventh-day Sabbath to a first day "Lord's Day" assemblage, took place by the Second Century C.E. so that the emerging Christian

---

[13] J.C. McCann, "Sabbath," in Geoffrey Bromiley, ed., *International Standard Bible Encyclopedia*, 4 vols. (Grand Rapids: Eerdmans, 1988), 4:252

Lengthy analyses of Colossians 2:16-23; Romans 14; Galatians 4:9-11; Acts 20:7-12; 1 Corinthians 16:1-2; and Revelation 1:10 are available in the **Sabbath and Rest in the Apostolic Scriptures** section of the *Messianic Sabbath Helper*.

[14] "the day of the Everpresent Lord" (The Messianic Writings).

[15] For a further examination, consult the relevant sections of the *Messianic Sabbath Helper*.

Church could establish an identity independent of the Jewish Synagogue. **This was the first stage of loss for the seventh-day Sabbath.** The *Dictionary of Judaism in the Biblical Period* describes, "Their desire for self-identification, the tradition of Jesus' Sunday morning resurrection, and the increasingly gentile church's disinterest in the Jewish Sabbath ritual led Christians eventually to designate Sunday as their day of worship."[16] *The Jewish Annotated New Testament* concurs that this took place "to commemorate the proclamation of Jesus' resurrection and to distinguish its practices from that of the synagogue."[17] While it is historically undeniable that various pockets of Christians were keeping Sunday as "the Lord's Day" by the early Second Century—whether such a change was, in fact, legitimate by the second, and certainly third generation, Apostolic successors should and has been challenged. In the estimation of MacCarty,

"This is not to deny that Jesus' resurrection was a cataclysmic event in the history of salvation and that some form of at least annual celebration in remembrance of it would be natural for Christ's followers, even though Jesus did not institute it...But to establish weekly worship on the first day of the week, even for such worthy motives as celebrating the resurrection, to the abandonment of observing the seventh-day Sabbath commanded in Exod 20:8-11, is...unscriptural both in doctrine and practice."[18]

Even though MacCarty is a Seventh-Day Adventist, his conclusions would tend to be welcomed by Messianic people. In his *Jewish New Testament Commentary* remarks on Revelation 1:10, supportive of *tē Kuriakē hēmera* being "the Day of the Lord," David H. Stern asserts, "Ignatius, who claimed to be a disciple of the emissary Yochanan [John], wrote letters only two decades or so after Revelation was written, in which he uses '*kuriakê*' to mean Sunday—as does modern Greek. This only shows how quickly the Jewish roots of the New Testament were forgotten or ignored."[19]

---

[16] "Sabbath," in *Dictionary of Judaism in the Biblical Period*, 538.

[17] Amy-Jill Levine and Marc Zvi Brettler, eds., *The Jewish Annotated New Testament*, NRSV (Oxford: Oxford University Press, 2011), 615.

[18] MacCarty, "The Seventh-Day Sabbath," in *Perspectives on the Sabbath: Four Views*, 44.

[19] David H. Stern, *Jewish New Testament Commentary* (Clarksville, MD: Jewish New Testament Publications, 1992), 791.

Early Christian literature from the late First to Second Centuries is fairly deduced to be broad and diverse, but is also a proverbial "mixed bag," if you will. The early Christian writings give ample attestation to how many of these Believers were under intense persecution from the Roman authorities, and were facing the pressure of dangerous heresies such as Gnosticism. What is also witnessed, however, is a wide degree of misunderstanding, if not outright rejection, of much of Judaism and Torah practice. Far from various Christian leaders of the late First, and certainly into the Second Century, *changing* the Sabbath from Saturday to Sunday—the seventh-day Sabbath was *dismissed*, the concept of rest was *widely allegorized or spiritualized* to be a condition that Believers in Christ experience, and *a new "Lord's Day" of Sunday* was believed to be ideal for corporate worship.[20]

A selection of quotations from early Christian materials from the late First to late Second Century will frequently, but not always, include various negative remarks about Judaism and the Jewish people:

> "On the Lord's own day gather together and break bread and give thanks, having first confessed your sins so that your sacrifice may be pure" (*Didache* 14:1; late First-early Second Century C.E.).[21]

> "If, then, those who had lived according to ancient practices came to the newness of hope, no longer keeping the sabbath but living in accordance with the Lord's day, on which our life also arose through him and his death (which some deny), the mystery through which we came to believe, and because of which we patiently endure, in order that we may be found to be disciples of Jesus Christ, our only teacher...It is utterly absurd to profess Jesus Christ and to practice Judaism. For Christianity did not believe in Judaism, but Judaism in Christianity, in which every tongue believed and was brought

---

[20] Cf. "Sabbath," in David W. Bercot, ed., *A Dictionary of Early Christian Beliefs* (Peabody, MA: Hendrickson, 1998), pp 571-572.

[21] Michael W. Holmes, ed. and trans., *The Apostolic Fathers: Greek Texts and English Translations*, third edition (Grand Rapids: Baker Academic, 2007), 365.

together to God" (Ignatius *To the Magnesians* 9:1; 10:3; early Second Century C.E.).[22]

"Finally, he says to them: 'I cannot stand your new moons and sabbaths' [Isaiah 1:13]. You see what he means: it is not the present sabbaths that are acceptable to me, but the one that I have made; on that sabbath, after I have set everything at rest, I will create the beginning of an eighth day, which is the beginning of another world. This is why we spend the eighth day in celebration, the day on which Jesus both arose from the dead and, after appearing again, ascended into heaven" (*Epistle of Barnabas* 15:8-9; late First-early Second Century C.E.).[23]

"The new law requires you to keep perpetual sabbath, and you, because you are idle for one day, suppose you are pious...The Lord our God does not take pleasure in such observances...let him repent; then he has kept the sweet and true sabbaths of God" (Justin Martyr *Dialogue with Trypho* 12; mid-Second Century C.E.).[24]

"'There are such people, Trypho,' I answered; 'and these do not venture to have any intercourse with or to extend hospitality to such persons; but I do not agree with them. But if some, through weak-mindedness, wish to observe such institutions as were given by Moses, from which they expect some virtue, but which we believe were appointed by reason of the hardness of the people's hearts, along with their hope in this Christ, and [wish to perform] the eternal and natural acts of righteousness and piety, yet choose to live with the Christians and the faithful, as I said before, not inducing them either to be circumcised like themselves, or to keep the Sabbath, or to observe any other such ceremonies, then I hold that we ought to join ourselves to such, and associate with them in all things as kinsmen and brethren" (Justin Martyr *Dialogue with Trypho* 47; mid-Second Century C.E.).[25]

---

[22] Ibid., 209.

[23] Ibid., 429.

[24] BibleWorks 9.0: Schaff, Early Church Fathers. MS Windows 7 Release. Norfolk: BibleWorks, LLC, 2011. DVD-ROM.

[25] Ibid.

"...But the Sabbaths taught that we should continue day by day in God's service..." (Irenaeus *Against Heresies* 4.16.1; late Second Century C.E.).[26]

"...we neither accord with the Jews in their peculiarities in regard to food, nor in their sacred days, nor even in their well-known bodily sign, nor in the possession of a common name, which surely behoved to be the case if we did homage to the same God as they..." (Tertullian *Apology* 21; late Second Century C.E.).[27]

"...in so far as the abolition of carnal circumcision and of the old law is demonstrated as having been consummated at its specific times, so also the observance of the Sabbath is demonstrated to have been temporary" (Tertullian *An Answer to the Jews* 4; late Second Century C.E.).[28]

"The Holy Spirit upbraids the Jews with their holy-days. 'Your Sabbaths, and new moons, and ceremonies,' says He, 'My soul hateth' [Isaiah 1:13-14]. By us, to whom Sabbaths are strange, and the new moons and festivals formerly beloved by God, the Saturnalia and New-year's and Midwinter's festivals and Matronalia are frequented—presents come and go—New-year's gifts—games join their noise—banquets join their din! Oh better fidelity of the nations to their own sect, which claims no solemnity of the Christians for itself! Not the Lord's day, not Pentecost, even it they had known them, would they have shared with us; for they would fear lest they should seem to be Christians. *We* are not apprehensive lest we seem to be *heathens*! If any indulgence is to be granted to the flesh, you have it" (Tertullian *On Idolatry*; late Second Century C.E.).[29]

Some of the statements which are witnessed to deride the seventh-day Sabbath are also made in conjunction with dismissals of the appointed times or *moedim* (מוֹעֲדִים), circumcision,[30] and may

---

[26] Ibid.

[27] Ibid.

[28] Ibid.

[29] Ibid.

[30] Consult the article "Is Circumcision for Everyone?" by J.K. McKee, appearing in *Torah In the Balance, Volume II*.

have even included a misapplication of Isaiah 1:13.[31] Other statements, such as those of Justin Martyr, while dismissing the seventh-day Sabbath, do recognize that those Jewish Believers who kept the seventh-day Sabbath were not to be treated as pariahs, but were to be accepted as genuine, albeit weak, brethren. Tertullian is particularly bad, as his dismissal of the Sabbath and appointed times permitted concourse with heathenism.

Could one honestly see any of the Jewish Apostles of Yeshua of Nazareth say anything like what appears above? About as close as things might seemingly get would be Paul in Philippians 3:2-9,[32] but there Paul is seen comparing and contrasting his human achievements in Judaism, to what the Divine Messiah has achieved, and how faith in Yeshua brings redemption. Paul is not negative toward Judaism in Philippians 3:2-9, but in a perceived human status that can get people's attention off of what Yeshua has accomplished. Paul himself expressed that there was indeed edifying value in Judaism and Torah practice (Romans 3:1-2).

Much of the anti-Sabbath polemic witnessed in the emerging Christian Church of the Second Century, likely arose because of associations of Greek and Roman Christian Believers with either Judaism, or various pockets of Jewish Believers, who had then been largely pressured to leave and were excised because of the forces of history. This was widely consequent of the Jewish Revolt of 70 C.E. in Judea, and with it renewed anti-Semitism in the Roman Empire. The Apostles and some of their immediate successors were

---

[31] Isaiah 1:13 is examined in the **Sabbath and Rest in the Tanach** section of the *Messianic Sabbath Helper*.

[32] "Beware of the dogs, beware of the evil workers, beware of the mutilation; for we are the circumcision, who worship by the Spirit of God and glory in Messiah Yeshua and have no confidence in the flesh, though I myself might have confidence even in the flesh. If anyone else thinks to have confidence in the flesh, I far more: circumcised the eighth day, of the race of Israel, of the tribe of Benjamin, a Hebrew of Hebrews; as to the Torah, a Pharisee; as to zeal, persecuting the assembly; as to the righteousness which is in the Torah, found blameless. But whatever things were gain to me, these have I counted as loss for the sake of Messiah. But even more so, I count all things to be loss for the surpassing value of the knowledge of Messiah Yeshua my Lord, for whom I suffered the loss of all things, and count them but refuse in order that I may gain Messiah, and be found in Him, not having a righteousness of my own from the Torah, but that which is through the faithfulness of Messiah, the righteousness which is from God on the basis of faith" (Philippians 3:2-9, PME).

gone, and a new generation had emerged on the scene, which did not feel great kinship toward the Jewish people. A dismissal of the seventh-day Sabbath and its rest, superseded by Sunday "Lord's Day" gatherings, would help establish the Christians as being different from Judaism. Many Protestant Christians consider this course of history to have been God-directed.

Others, such as this writer—especially today with the emergence of Messianic Judaism on the scene—would see the Second Century as including what Paul recognized as, "For the mystery of lawlessness is already at work" (2 Thessalonians 2:7a). The roots and origins of our Messiah faith are the mixed Jewish and non-Jewish congregations of the First Century C.E., to which many of today's evangelical Christians are steadily returning. The roots and origins of our Messiah faith are not Second Century assemblies that wanted little or nothing to do with Judaism and the Jewish people; such Second Century Christians made a number of lamentable mistakes.[33]

Sunday Mandated as Religious Day

While there was a dismissal of the seventh-day Sabbath by many leaders of the emerging Christian Church of the Second Century C.E., the Roman Emperor Constantine is witnessed as having made Sunday or the first day a mandated religious day, as a part of his presumed conversion to Christianity in the Fourth Century C.E. As is witnessed in the historical record, Constantine's conversion to Christianity did play a definite role in the consolidation of his political power as emperor of the Eastern Roman Empire, neutralizing the aristocratic families of Rome who followed the old gods, and the construction of his new capital at Byzantium.

---

[33] That the late First and early Second Centuries C.E. included negative events, by which the Body of Messiah was severed from much of its heritage in the Jewish Synagogue, with the Jewish people believed to be inferior to the Christians (among other things), does not go unnoticed by various evangelical Christian theologians.

Consult the useful summary offered in Walter C. Kaiser, *Recovering the Unity of the Bible: One Continuous Story, Plan, and Purpose* (Grand Rapids: Zondervan, 2009), pp 221-222. Kaiser credits D. Thomas Lancaster, *Restoration: Returning the Torah of God to the Disciples of Jesus* (Littleton, CO: First Fruits of Zion, 2005), pp 13-28 on being influential to his discussion.

The first day or Sunday had significance for the Christians who observed Sunday as "the Lord's Day," and it also had significance for many of the pagans as well. Philip Schaff, author of the significant work *History of the Christian Church*, informs us, "He enjoined the observance, or rather forbade the public desecration of Sunday, not under the name of *Sabbatum* or *Dies Domini*, but under its old astrological and heathen title, *Dies Solis*, familiar to all his subjects, so that the law was as applicable to the worshippers of Hercules, Apollo, and Mithras, as to the Christians."[34] As is noted, the decree issued on 07 March, 321 C.E. legislated Sunday or the first day of the week, as a civil ordinance, requiring a cessation of business in urban areas:

"On the venerable Day of the Sun let the magistrates and people residing in cities rest, and let all workshops be closed. In the country, however, persons engaged in agriculture may freely and lawfully continue their pursuits; because it often happens that another day is not so suitable for grain-sowing or for vine-planting; lest by neglecting the proper moment for such operations the bounty of heaven should be lost."[35]

The Emperor Constantine did not change the seventh-day Sabbath to Sunday for the Christians of his time, as many of the Christians were already observing a Sunday "Lord's Day" which was, albeit errantly, believed to have superseded the Sabbath. The Emperor Constantine did declare Sunday a civil day for religious observance, which had the advantage of being a day employed by both the Christians and the pagans.

There has certainly been a great deal of ink spilled on the mandate of the first day of the week as a religious day by the decree of Constantine, some of which has embellished the issue of Sunday far beyond what is reasonable *and* what is provable. During my studies at Asbury Theological Seminary (2005-2009), two of the major textbooks I was assigned for Church History I (Summer 2005), certainly provided a reasoned approach to what Constantine's adoption of Christianity meant to the Fourth Century bifurcated Roman Empire, the civil decree involving Sunday, and

---

[34] Philip Schaff, *History of the Christian Church: Nicene and Post-Nicene Christianity*, Vol III (Grand Rapids: Eerdmans, 1910/1995), 380.

[35] Ibid., fn#1.

the merging of political and ecclesiastical power structures (*The Story of Christianity*, Vol. 1[36]; *History of the World Christian Movement*, Vol 1[37]). Information, on the Emperor Constantine and his syncretism, is not difficult to find, and will often be encountered by those being trained as contemporary pastors and teachers in modern Protestantism.

It is fair to deduce that the Emperor Constantine had an agenda when professing himself to be a "Christian." While what is seen in later history, started with Constantine, how imperial and ecclesiastical power structures merged—something later negatively epitomized in the hierarchy of the Roman Catholic Church of the Middle Ages—Constantine did not change the Sabbath to Sunday. Instead, as the *Dictionary of Theological Terms* concludes, "He *enforced* the observance of the first day of the week, a very different thing from *commencing* it."[38] The first day of the week, or Sunday, bore some significance for the pagans, as well as the Christians who had widely already jettisoned *Shabbat*. Constantine, in our modern terms, rubber stamped *a common day of religious activity* for both the pagans and Christians in his realm.

More problematic is that the religious councils, which began meeting subsequent to Christianity being legalized, did in fact declare it illegal for Christians to associate with members of the Jewish community, for both the Passover and the seventh-day Sabbath. **This is what constitutes the second stage of loss for the Sabbath.**

The Council of Antioch (341 C.E.) decreed that anyone caught celebrating the Lord's resurrection ("Easter") at the same time as the Jewish Passover would be excommunicated from the Church, and be considered to be causing destruction to his soul:

> But if any one of those who preside in the Church, whether he be bishop, presbyter, or deacon, shall presume, after this decree, to exercise his own private judgment to the subversion of the people and to the disturbance of the churches, by

---

[36] Justo L. González, *The Story of Christianity*, Vol. 1 (San Francisco: Harper Collins, 1984), pp 121-123.

[37] Dale T. Irvin and Scott W. Sunquist, *History of the World Christian Movement*, Vol. 1 (Maryknoll, NY: Orbis Books, 2001), pp 161-164.

[38] "Sabbath," in *Dictionary of Theological Terms*, 393.

> observing Easter [at the same time] with the Jews, the holy Synod decrees that he shall thenceforth be an alien from the Church, as one who not only heaps sins upon himself, but who is also the cause of destruction and subversion to many; and it deposes not only such persons themselves from their ministry, but those also who after their deposition shall presume to communicate with them (Canon 1).[39]

The Council of Laodicea (363 C.E.) decreed that Christians should not rest on the Sabbath, but instead observe "the Lord's Day":

> Here the Fathers order that no one of the faithful shall stop work on the Sabbath as do the Jews, but that they should honor the Lord's Day; on account of the Lord's resurrection, and that on that day they should abstain from manual labor and go to church. But thus abstaining from work on Sunday they do not lay down as a necessity, but they add, 'if they can.' For if through need or any other necessity any one worked on the Lord's day this was not reckoned against him (Canon 29).[40]

Such a dismissal of the seventh-day Sabbath, by the leaders of Fourth Century Christendom, is hardly a positive development, as it surely involved further merging and consolidation of imperial authority and spiritual control, here undoubtedly tempered by some anti-Semitism as well. In *Recovering the Unity of the Bible*, Kaiser notes the problems caused by these councils:

"When Emperor Constantine converted to Christianity and made it a legal religion in the empire, he had the divorce between Judaism and Christianity final with the Council of Nicea (AD 325). His estimate of the Torah was 'let us have nothing in common with the detestable Jewish rabble' [Eusebius, *Life of Constantine* 3:18-19]. The Council of Antioch (AD 341) followed suit by forbidding Christians from celebrating Passover with the Jews, and the Council of Laodicea (AD 363) forbade Christians from celebrating the seventh-day Sabbath. But it is clear that all the way up to the

[39] *The Post-Nicene Fathers*, P. Schaff, ed.; Libronix Digital Library System 1.0d: Church History Collection. MS Windows XP. Garland, TX: Galaxie Software. 2002.

[40] Ibid.

fourth century of the Christian era some believers were still keeping parts of the Torah."[41]

Sabbath in the Reformation and Post-Reformation

It should hardly be surprising that with the merger of imperial and ecclesiastical power via the reign of Constantine, extending all the way into European Christianity via the Roman Catholic Church, that issues pertaining to the first day of the week and what role, if any, the seventh-day Sabbath might have for Christians, **did not become pronounced again until the Protestant Reformation.** With the Reformation, and Christians in Europe being able to access the Bible in their native languages, did issues surrounding Sabbatarianism get revisited. A fairly broad approach to the issue of Sabbatarianism, that arose in European Protestantism, and later Great Britain and its colonies, is noted by J. Parton Payne in *Baker's Dictionary of Theology:*

"Luther rejected sabbath-keeping...but the Puritans established England's comprehensive sabbath law of 1677. The Scottish and colonial 'blue-laws' are today being increasingly relaxed or eliminated."[42]

For many Protestant Christians, Sunday was the Christian Sabbath, and such a transfer was believed to have been authorized by the Apostles. There were, though, various early Reformers which did not support Sabbath keeping of any kind, and instead allegorized or spiritualized it like many of the Second Century figures who dismissed *Shabbat*. There were various Christians in Silesia and Moravia, during the early days of the Reformation in the 1520s, observing the seventh-day Sabbath, and were fiercely opposed by Martin Luther. Some of the Sabbatarians of the mid-to-late Sixteenth Century were Unitarians, being unsure, at best, on the Divine nature of the Messiah.[43]

---

[41] Kaiser, *Recovering the Unity of the Bible*, pp 222-223.

[42] J. Barton Payne, "Sabbatarianism," in Everett F. Harrison, ed., *Baker's Dictionary of Theology* (Grand Rapids: Baker Book House, 1960), 464.

[43] F.R. Harm, "Sabbatarianism," in Walter A. Elwell, *Evangelical Dictionary of Theology* (Grand Rapids: Baker Academic, 2001), 1045; Judith Shulevitz, *The Sabbath World: Glimpses of a Different Order of Time* (New York: Random House, 2010), pp 128-130.

By the Seventeenth and Eighteenth Centuries, particularly in Britain—influenced by a conflux of Reformed theology, Puritanism, and even the later Wesleyan movement—Sunday was widely set aside for the Christian day of worship and rest. Still, there were others, such as the Seventh-Day Baptists, but most notably the Seventh-Day Adventists in the Nineteenth Century, who did help to revive the seventh-day Sabbath:

> "It was not until the 4th cent. that Sunday began to take on Sabbath characteristics, when Constantine decreed that certain types of work should not be done on Sunday. This sabbatarian tendency continued over the next several centuries until the Decretals of Gregory XI (A.D. 1234) officially mandated Sunday rest. The Protestant Reformation represented a reversal, with the Reformers tending to spiritualize the sabbath commandments and to argue that any day of the week could be set aside for worship and rest. The inheritors of the Reformation tradition generally returned to a sabbatarian position, due in part to the prevalence of biblical literalism in the 17th through 19th centuries. The most literal interpreters advocated a seventh-day sabbatarianism. A return to seventh-day sabbatarianism had begun among some sixteenth-century Anabaptists, and this tradition has been carried into the present by English and American Seventh-Day Baptists and by Seventh-Day Adventism, which arose in America in the 19th century" (*ISBE*).[44]

Many of us in the Messianic movement, from evangelical Protestant backgrounds, have been affected by past generations of our family keeping some form of "Sunday Sabbath." The keeping of a rigid Sunday Sabbath, if you live in Great Britain or in one of its former colonies, is something widely inherited from Seventeenth Century Puritanism,[45] and then the spiritual movements it immediately affected. Later piety movements of the Eighteenth and into the Nineteenth Centuries tended to stress a "Sunday Sabbath,"

---

[44] McCann, "Sabbath," in *ISBE*, 4:252.

Harm, "Sabbatarianism," in *Evangelical Dictionary of Theology*, 1045 further states, "The Seventh-day Baptists originated in 1631, bringing sabbatarianism to England and later to Rhode Island and New York. The most notable proponent of strict sabbatarianism at the present time is the Seventh-day Adventist Church."

[45] Shulevitz, pp 138-150.

in observance of the Fourth Commandment, as a necessity for Christian people. Sunday was the day to go to church, to not do any laborious work, to not engage in commerce, and to spend time reading the Scriptures and interacting with one's family and fellow Christians. F.R. Harm labels this in the *Evangelical Dictionary of Theology* to actually be "Semisabbatarianism":

"Semisabbatarianism holds a view essentially the same as strict sabbatarianism but transfers its demands from Saturday, the seventh day, to Sunday, the first day of the week...Semisabbatarianism reached its zenith in English Puritanism, later finding its way to the New World through the early colonists. Sunday restrictions and so-called blue laws in various states are a constant reminder of the influence of this view on the laws of our land."[46]

How did many Protestants come to the conclusion that the seventh-day Sabbath was changed to the first day of Sunday, believed to be "the Lord's Day"? As is witnessed in Reformation period history, such a conclusion was not reached by consulting Roman Catholic authorities, but instead by seeing New Testament passages such as 1 Corinthians 16:1-2 and Acts 20:7, about Believers meeting on the first of the week, in conjunction with the practice of many Christians of the Second Century C.E. As is witnessed in the Westminster Confession, a huge array of doctrinal tenets and theological constructs for the Reformed tradition, some significant Tanach or Old Testament stipulations surrounding *Shabbat* are directly applied to Sunday as the "Christian Sabbath":

> "As it is the law of nature, that, in general, a due proportion of time be set apart for the worship of God; so, in His Word, by a positive, moral, and perpetual commandment binding all men in all ages, He hath particularly appointed one day in seven, for a Sabbath, to be kept holy unto Him [Exodus 20:8,10,11; Isaiah 56:2,4,6,7]: which, from the beginning of the world to the resurrection of Christ, was the last day of the week; and, from the resurrection of Christ, was changed into the first day of the week [Genesis 2:2,3; 1 Corinthians 16:1,2;

[46] Harm, "Sabbatarianism," in *Evangelical Dictionary of Theology*, 1045.

Cf. Shulevitz, pp 193-194 for a summary of how Sunday blue laws still affect parts of the United States today.

> Acts 20:7], which, in Scripture, is called the Lord's Day [Revelation 1:10], and is to be continued to the end of the world, as the Christian Sabbath [Exodus 20:8,10; Matthew 5:17,18].
>
> "This Sabbath is then kept holy unto the Lord, when men, after a due preparing of their hearts, and ordering of their common affairs beforehand, do not only observe an holy rest, all the day, from their own works, words, and thoughts about their worldly employments and recreations [Exodus 20:8; 16:23,25,26,29,30; 31:15; Nehemiah 13:15-19,21,22]; but also are taken up, the whole time, in the public and private exercises of His worship, and in the duties of necessity and mercy [Isaiah 58:13; Matthew 12:1-13]" (21.7-8).[47]

In the customary Reformed division of the Torah or Law of Moses into the presumed "moral law," "civil law," and "ceremonial law," the fact that Sabbath violation in the Pentateuch frequently brought with it capital punishment—was believed to make the Sabbath a moral law. Reading in Scripture that the Believers held some kind of meeting on the "first of the week," and not thinking through the Jewish reckoning of time, among other things, they thought it fair to deduce that the Apostles shifted the Sabbath to Sunday. Hebrews 4:9 might have even been appealed to, "So there remains a Sabbath rest for the people of God," with this representing a new Sunday Sabbath[48] (as opposed to a future eschatological rest, typified by the weekly seventh-day Sabbath).[49] While some of the arguments made by Protestant Christians of the past observing a "Sunday Sabbath" are disengaged from a First Century Jewish background of the Holy Scriptures, today's Messianic people should be fair enough to recognize that **a Sunday Sabbath is better than no Sabbath at all.** Many Christians, of the Second and Third Centuries, and of the Reformation and post-Reformation, have thought that the Sabbath rest is to be totally allegorized and spiritualized as a condition they experience in the Messiah, and that a physical Sabbath rest is of little use.

---

[47] BibleWorks 9.0: Westminster Standards.

[48] Cf. Joseph A. Pipa, "The Christian Sabbath," in *Perspectives on the Sabbath: Four Views*, 165.

[49] Hebrews 4:1-10 is examined in the **Sabbath and Rest in the Apostolic Scriptures** section of the *Messianic Sabbath Helper*.

Over the past two centuries, to be sure, questions have been raised by many Christian people about the Sabbath, and specifically about whether the seventh-day Sabbath does indeed have validity and relevance for all of God's people. MacCarty, a Seventh-Day Adventist pastor, poses the inquiry, "While the earlier Reformers had other battles to fight with the Church of Rome, once the Reformation began, it was inevitable that there would be a controversy over the identity of the true Sabbath. We believe that time is well past due."[50]

Today's broad Messianic movement is obviously in a unique position, because it inherits a faith tradition directly from Judaism, with even the most liberal Jews from the Reform Synagogue keeping some sort of *Shabbat* observance on the seventh-day. Yet, today's Messianic movement also does inherit a faith tradition from evangelical Protestantism. Leaders and people alike—and not just non-Jewish Believers in the Messianic movement, but Jewish Believers who were either raised in Protestantism and then became part of a new Messianic Jewish movement, or have been trained in Protestant seminaries—have been influenced by a diverse array of evangelical theologies on the Sabbath. This includes: Baptist and Presbyterian Calvinism, Wesleyan-Arminianism and Methodism, as well as the Pentecostal and charismatic movements. All of these sectors, at one point or another, among others, have been influenced by what has been labeled as Semisabbatarianism.

In present Messianic observance of the weekly *Shabbat* on the seventh-day (Saturday), the Semisabbatarianism, of past Protestant Christians, might actually need to be consulted to some degree. While Messianic Believers do observe the Sabbath on the correct day, past generations of Believers did desire to sanctify a day as holy unto God, abstaining from their labors, and resting in Him. *And, God surely blessed them for their obedient intentions.* Much of how they did this, even though it was on Sunday, was likely much more focused and regimented than how many Messianics today keep *Shabbat*.

[50] MacCarty, "The Seventh-Day Sabbath," in *Perspectives on the Sabbath: Four Views*, 46.

How do we recover the Sabbath?

Many of us, Jewish and non-Jewish alike, have been led into today's emerging Messianic movement, in these early days of our growth and development, and have received a sense from the Lord that He is preparing us to do some very vital and important work before the Messiah's return. It is being heard in increasing numbers, *"This is the end-time move of God!"* As we approach the return of Yeshua, it should not at all be surprising that the future, worldwide Sabbath observance, to be experienced during His Millennial reign (Isaiah 66:23), is more consciously breaking into the hearts and minds of His people.

Not enough in today's Messianic community are probably aware of this, but many of today's contemporary Christian people are aware of how total dismissal of the Sabbath-principle and its concept of rest have not at all aided Believers. *If for any other reason, that Believers need to stop their activities and rest for a day, should help the stress level and health problems that beset far too many.* But more than this, a variety of key publications, mostly by evangelical Christians wanting to recapture the Sunday Sabbath of their ancestors, have been released into the marketplace of ideas.[51] **That many of today's Christians want to observe a Sabbath rest is a good thing.** Some have even tried out a seventh-day Sabbath on Saturday![52]

A perfect storm, as some would say, is on the horizon. Today's Messianic movement needs to recognize that in this hour, the Lord can surely use renewed Christian interest in the Sabbath—to see many of our fellow brothers and sisters exposed not only to

---

[51] These publications include, but are not limited to:

Marva J. Dawn, *Keeping the Sabbath Wholly: Ceasing, Resting, Embracing, Feasting* (Grand Rapids: Eerdmans, 1989); Wayne Muller, *Sabbath: Finding Rest, Renewal, and Delight in Our Busy Lives* (New York: Bantam Books, 1999); Norman Wirzba, *Living the Sabbath: Discovering the Rhythms of Rest and Delight* (Grand Rapids: Brazos Press, 2006); Mark Buchanan, *The Rest of God: Restoring Your Soul by Restoring Sabbath* (Nashville: W Publishing Group, 2006); Dan B. Allender, *Sabbath* (Nashville: Thomas Nelson, 2009); Keri Wyatt Kent, *Rest: Living in Sabbath Simplicity* (Grand Rapids: Zondervan, 2009); Walter Brueggemann, *Sabbath as Resistance: Saying No to the Culture of Now* (Louisville: Westminster John Knox, 2014).

[52] See Lisa Gleaves, *Claim God's Sabbath Blessings! "What God's Word Says About Sabbath"* (2013) [eBook for Amazon Kindle].

Shabbat as we know it, but also the appointed times, and their faith heritage in the Hebrew Tanach and in Judaism. We can indeed see a style of faith emerge that is similar to that of the early Jewish, Greek, and Roman Believers who composed some of the early assemblies out in the Mediterranean. We cannot alter what happened in the past when the Sabbath was lost, **but we can enact a future where the weekly Sabbath is recovered and appreciated.** The *willingness to change* is definitely present on the part of many of today's sincere, seeking men and women—but this must also be enjoined with a willingness on the part of today's Messianic people *to welcome*.

How Do We Properly Keep Shabbat?

How the Messianic community is to properly keep *Shabbat*, or any Biblical commandment for that matter, is a mystery for many. There are many issues and questions that have to be weighed and taken into consideration when establishing a proper *halachic* orthopraxy for oneself, one's congregation, and the movement as a whole. In the Jewish community, whether you are Orthodox or Conservative, keeping the seventh-day Sabbath is an important sign of who you are as a Jew. It is the sign that God gave the people of Israel from Mount Sinai to distinguish them from the world. When one goes to Israel today, stores close, public transportation stops, and the Old City of Jerusalem comes to a virtual standstill for a full twenty-four hours. When some in the emerging Messianic movement see how our Jewish brothers and sisters keep the Sabbath, it can seem almost foreboding and something that needs to be minimized. When our Christian brethren see how Orthodox Jews keep the Sabbath, they often run away, believing it to be a time of forced "unwork," legalism, and anything but rest.

But as you can imagine, this is not what God originally intended. The Lord gave us the gift of *Shabbat* so that we might rest and abstain from our labors, focus exclusively on Him, and be rejuvenated for the week of work ahead. Yeshua the Messiah tells us, "The sabbath was made for humankind, and not humankind for the Sabbath" (Mark 2:27, NRSV). God gave *Shabbat* to all people so that it would be a special time for us, not a time that is burdensome or intended to place men and women into bondage. He asks us to "Sanctify My sabbaths; and they shall be a sign between Me and you, that you may know that I am the LORD your God" (Ezekiel

20:20). Anything surrounding *Shabbat* is to be focused on this end: the Sabbath is to be a time so that we might "know" the Lord. *Yada* (יָדַע) is a common verb in Biblical Hebrew not only used to describe knowledge, but most importantly is "used for the most intimate acquaintance" (*TWOT*).[1] On *Shabbat*, we are to be intimate with our Heavenly Father, and with other Believers in the community of faith.

While those of us who have salvation in Yeshua, and have the gift of the Holy Spirit present inside us, should leap inside when we realize that the Sabbath is to be a time when we commune with our Father—how we keep *Shabbat* is another story. It begs many difficult questions. When many become convicted that Sunday Church is not what God originally intended, and that His people need to keep *Shabbat*, various changes begin to take place. The transition to *Shabbat* is difficult for many, especially given the many Christian misconceptions about what the seventh-day Sabbath is, and why God gave it to His people. While on paper many Messianic Believers say they keep the Biblical Sabbath—keeping *Shabbat* is not just transferring a Sunday Church experience to Saturday. While the Sabbath has elements of worshipping God involved with it, *Shabbat* is not about "worshipping on Saturday." It is, rather, one of the appointed times or *moedim* of Leviticus 23. It is to be "a sacred occasion" (NJPS) or "a sacred assembly" (NIV). But being these things involves much more than just worship:

"For six days work may be done, but on the seventh day there is a sabbath of complete rest, a holy convocation. You shall not do any work; it is a sabbath to the LORD in all your dwellings" (Leviticus 23:3).

The question of *why we need to keep the Sabbath* is fairly easy to answer. Our Heavenly Father wants us to abstain from our labors. Exodus 20:11 attests, "For in six days the LORD made the heavens and the earth, the sea and all that is in them, and rested on the seventh day; therefore the LORD blessed the sabbath day and made it holy." The verb *nuach* (נוּחַ), appearing here in the Qal stem (simple action, active voice), means to "*rest, settle down and*

---

[1] Jack P. Lewis, "ידע," in *TWOT*, 1:366.

remain" (*BDB*).[2] Every week, we need to just stop what we are doing, and "settle down" for a while. We need to abstain from our labors and stop working. However, there is a great amount of discussion concerning what it actually means to *stop working*. Keeping the Sabbath is a wonderful thing—but how are we to keep it properly? How do we not forget the essence and joy of *Shabbat*, but at the same time not eliminating its primary aims?

What do we have to consider?

We as the emerging Messianic community today have a substantial amount to consider when we contemplate *how we are to properly keep the Sabbath*. We have to make some serious ideological and philosophical value judgments, and also weigh our testimony to both our Christian and Jewish brethren, and sometimes our Messianic Jewish brethren, if we are non-Jewish. We have to answer some serious questions relating to our individual and corporate callings, and what we believe that God is trying to achieve through our obedience to Him. We have to ask ourselves if we want to alienate ourselves from others, or let others be drawn toward us because we are truly being blessed by obeying the Lord. We also have to allow for some flexibility among those who keep *Shabbat*, because not everyone is going to keep it exactly the same way that we are.

I believe that there are three critical questions that we all have to consider as we contemplate how we are to properly keep *Shabbat*. Obviously as you will see below, these questions do not exclusively relate to the Sabbath, but for our specific purposes, we will assume that they are:

1. How am I to keep *Shabbat* as an individual?
2. How is my congregation or fellowship to keep *Shabbat?*
3. How are we to keep *Shabbat* as the Messianic community, and are we trying to emulate Jewish practice in any respect?

How you answer these questions will affect how you interpret the Biblical commandments regarding the seventh-day Sabbath. There are many people in the Messianic community today who say

[2] *BDB*, 628.

that they keep *Shabbat*, but then we have those in our midst who accuse such people of not keeping the Sabbath, because they do not keep the Sabbath as "they do." Consider the fact that while the Written Torah absolutely prohibits work from being done on *Shabbat*, what one person considers work, another person might not consider work. While the commandments themselves are not what are in dispute among Messianic Believers who believe that *Shabbat* is to be observed—their application is. This begs the questions of not only how we are to develop an individual *halachah* of how the Sabbath is to be kept, but to what degree, if any, the emerging Messianic movement considers Jewish tradition and commentary regarding *Shabbat*.

One of the things that I think many non-Jewish Believers in the Messianic movement do not realize is that salvation has gone out into the nations, so that non-Jewish Believers might provoke their Jewish brethren to faith in Yeshua. Paul writes this in Romans 11:11, "Again I ask: Did they stumble so as to fall beyond recovery? Not at all! Rather, because of their transgression, salvation has come to the Gentiles to make Israel envious" (NIV). Whatever non-Jewish Believers do regarding their Torah observance should make the Jewish people jealous. This should be because they see non-Jewish Believers keeping "their Torah," and doing the things that "they are supposed to do." I can tell you from personal experience that those who are the most jealous, of families like mine, are non-religious or nominally-religious Jews. When they see a non-Jewish Believer, a "Christian" in their minds, keeping the things of the Torah, they get extremely offended. They get offended because they know that *they should be doing these things*, and have decided instead not to do them. According to Paul, these things need to make our Jewish brothers and sisters *jealous for faith in the Messiah!*

But what can happen, and what often does happen, is that in much of the Messianic movement, many non-Jewish Believers think that they "know better" than Judaism in regard to the Torah. Hence, we have seen many interpretations and applications of Torah commandments that are foreign to the mainline Conservative and Orthodox Judaisms of today, and certainly to the Judaisms of the First Century. This can occur for any number of reasons, but notably because such non-Jewish Believers want to be

"Scripture Only" in the strictest sense of the term, and believe that the Jewish people have rejected Yeshua because of their own customs and traditions. In extreme cases, some non-Jewish Believers in the Messianic community are actually anti-Semitic.[3]

I believe these sentiments are misguided. The Protestant Reformers themselves, while believing in the primacy of written Scripture, never envisioned an interpretation of Scripture that did not take into consideration history and tradition, and for that same matter, reason and one's personal faith experience (or even one's own native culture). Secondly, the field of Jewish New Testament studies, which involve the examination of First Century history and literature, is revealing more and more that Yeshua the Messiah followed more of the traditions of Second Temple Judaism than He is commonly given credit for in most evangelical Christian exegesis. In fact, not only is scholastic opinion leaning more and more toward Yeshua keeping many of the oral traditions of the Rabbis, but it is being shaped by the fact that Yeshua's (and for that same matter, Paul's) theology is quite Pharisaical at its core. The foundation of Pharisaical theology is a belief in the bodily resurrection, an afterlife, angels, demons, miracles, and a compatibilist position of predestination and free will.[4]

In the case of *Shabbat*, many have decided to keep the Sabbath without considering any Jewish traditions or opinions concerning it. This is disconcerting because non-Jewish Believers will be unable to fulfill the call of provoking Jews to jealousy for faith in Yeshua if they follow the Torah without any Jewish elements present. While the statement of, "You don't want to come out of the Church and trade one set of traditions of men for another set of traditions of men," has become commonplace in certain parts of the Messianic community, and definitely in the independent Hebrew/Hebraic Roots movement—the simple fact of the matter is that traditions help bind a community together. Tradition has been what has kept the Jewish people bonded for almost two thousand years since the destruction of the Second Temple. Tradition is what allows a group

[3] Consult the thoughts summarized in "Anti-Semitism in the Two-House Movement," appearing in the book *Israel In Future Prophecy* by J.K. McKee.

[4] Consult the article "You Want to be a Pharisee," appearing in the *Messianic Torah Helper*, which more thoroughly explains this.

to formulate an established working opinion of how things are to be done. While "tradition" can be a "buzz word," in certain sectors, any objective reading of the Apostolic Scriptures, coupled with history, is revealing more and more that Yeshua and His early followers kept many of the Jewish traditions of their time. The Apostle Paul commended the Corinthians with the following word: "Now I praise you because you remember me in everything and hold firmly to the traditions, just as I delivered them to you" (1 Corinthians 11:2).[5] Should we not consult Jewish tradition when developing a viable *halachah* for ourselves?

I do not believe that the emerging Messianic community must follow all of the Jewish traditions that exist relating to *Shabbat*. In fact, there are many variances among the customs and traditions that exist, which have developed in different types of Jewish communities, i.e., the Ashkenazic or Sephardic communities, for hundreds of years. Some in the Messianic community want to act just like "Orthodox Jews." Is this something that we want? Many in the Orthodox Jewish community live and act like they live in Seventeenth Century Eastern Europe, and enclose themselves to not interact with society at large. Consequently, how the Sabbath is kept also needs to be tempered by the fact that we live in a modern world. The development and progress of technology has changed our ability to communicate, travel, and do things that in the ancient world, *especially the period of when the Torah was originally given*, was extremely difficult. When considering *how* the Sabbath is to be properly observed, we also have to weigh how much differently we live from the ancients. When consulting tradition, how much weight do we give to those Jewish sects who shut themselves off from the world, versus other Jewish sects which strive to be obedient to God in a modern world?

As we list the specific *Shabbat* prohibitions that Scripture gives us below, these are all factors that must be considered as we endeavor to have a viable Messianic *halachic* orthopraxy—not only for our individual selves, but also for our congregations, and for the movement at large. This is not intended to be a detailed exposition

---

[5] The Greek word *paradosis* (παράδοσις) specifically pertains to "tradition, of teachings, commandments, narratives et al.," and can refer to "the tradition of the rabbis" (*BDAG*, 763).

by any means, but attempts to offer practical solutions as to how we might keep the Sabbath as Messianic Believers in a modern world.

The Shabbat Prohibitions

Here are a collection of specific admonitions in Scripture as they relate to properly keeping *Shabbat*. These are the prohibitions that we will be examining, hopefully so that we can have a good idea about how God's people are to conduct ourselves on *Shabbat*, and how it is probably not as complicated as we often think it is.

1. The seventh day is the Sabbath, requiring a suspension of all labor.
2. The Sabbath is to be a holy convocation.
3. Work is to be done in the first six days of the week.
4. The Sabbath is to be a day of complete rest.
5. Fire shall not be kindled on the Sabbath.
6. On the Sabbath, God's people are to remember that the Ancient Israelites were once slaves in Egypt.
7. God's people are not to be concerned about their own carnal pleasures.
8. Conducting in business is prohibited on the Sabbath.

1. The seventh day is the Sabbath, requiring a suspension of all labor.

The Torah commands in Exodus 20:10, "the seventh day is a sabbath of the LORD your God; *in it* you shall not do any work, you or your son or your daughter, your male or your female servant or your cattle or your sojourner who stays with you." We are told the reason why God wants His people to abstain from their work in v. 11: "For in six days the LORD made the heavens and the earth, the sea and all that is in them, and rested on the seventh day; therefore the LORD blessed the sabbath day and made it holy." The purpose of *Shabbat* is so that we can remember God's supremacy as Creator, how He created the universe for His Divine purposes, and how when He had completed His work creating the universe, God rested. While some might argue, "How can a Supreme Being who controls the universe actually 'rest'?", the truth of the matter remains that God's ways are not our ways. The Lord moved upon human beings to write in corporeal terms infinitely more profound truths that we will not fully understand until we enter into His Kingdom and into eternity. But until that time, just as God ceased from the labor required to build the universe on the seventh day, so must we stop from our labors.

In the Hebrew Scriptures, the two words that are often used to describe "labor" are *avodah* (עֲבֹדָה), meaning "labor, service" (*BDB*), and its verb form, *avad* (עָבַד), generally meaning to "**work, serve**" (*BDB*).[6] These words are used in tandem in Exodus 1:13-14 to describe the harsh work that Pharaoh had the Ancient Israelites under while in Egypt:

"The Egyptians compelled the sons of Israel to labor [*avad*] rigorously; and they made their lives bitter with hard labor [*avodah*] in mortar and bricks and at all *kinds* of labor [*avodah*] in the field, all their labors which they rigorously imposed on them."

While this kind of work could certainly be in mind in the Sabbath prohibition given in the Decalogue, what is more specifically in mind is the type of work that brings financial gain. The prohibition given by God to Ancient Israel is that they are not to perform any *melakah* (מְלָאכָה). In the Hebrew Scriptures this has a wide variance of possible applications, including, "**trade mission, business journey**," "**business, work**," and "**handiwork, craftsmanship**" (*HALOT*).[7]

The challenge with properly interpreting the Fourth Commandment text given here is noted by Nahum M. Sarna: "The definition of prohibited labor (*m'lakhah*), which limits the commandment explicitly to creation (Gen 2:2), is not given here."[8] While the Fourth Commandment tells us that work is not to be done by anyone in the community, the types of specific work that are forbidden are not explained. This leaves the interpreter with one of two options when applying this text today: (1) examine further Scriptures that describe prohibitions of work on the

---

[6] *BDB*, pp 715, 712.

[7] *HALOT*, 1:586.

[8] Nahum M. Sarna, "Exodus," in David L. Lieber, ed., *Etz Hayim: Torah and Commentary* (New York: Rabbinical Assembly, 2001), 446.

Sabbath that build upon the Fourth Commandment, or (2) apply modern definitions of "work" to this Scripture.

The challenge, of course, with applying modern definitions of "work," i.e., "going to work," is that the largely agrarian society of the Ancient Israelites did not have the same concept of "work" as we often know it in the Western world today. The Ancient Israelites did not "go to jobs" and clock-in as employed workers from nine-to-five. They lived on their farms or functioned in a particular trade, and had a much less-definite view of "work." The First Century Jews for that same matter, even merchants in the Diaspora, did not consider "work" as we do. In applying this commandment in a Twenty-First Century model, we have to see how religious communities have applied it for their particular settings, and as Believers ask the Holy Spirit to show us how we can properly apply it today while maintaining the integrity of the prohibition not to "work."

2. The Sabbath is to be a holy convocation.

While the Torah identifies that the Sabbath is to be a time when God's people abstain from work, it is also listed in the series of appointed times or *moedim* that the Lord establishes for His people. Leviticus 23:3 attests, "For six days work may be done, but on the seventh day there is a sabbath of complete rest, a holy convocation. You shall not do any work; it is a sabbath to the LORD in all your dwellings." There are some Jewish scholars who do not believe that *Shabbat* should be considered one of the "appointed times," per se, arguing instead that if one simply keeps the Sabbath, then he or she will be naturally inclined to keep the high holidays of the Lord. This logic is valid, but regardless of one's view, Leviticus 23 says that *Shabbat* is "a day of sacred assembly" (NIV). What is this *miqra qodesh* (מִקְרָא־קֹדֶשׁ)?

The Hebrew word *miqra* generally means a "**summons**" or an "**assembly**" (*HALOT*).[9] It is derived from the verb *qara* (קָרָא), meaning "**call, proclaim, read**" (*BDB*).[10] It is from these various roots that the Jewish custom of assembling in a synagogue on *Shabbat* is derived. Nehemiah 8:8 indicates that this practice was

---

[9] *HALOT*, 1:629.

[10] *BDB*, 894.

developing after the Southern Kingdom exiles returned from Babylon: "They read [*qara*] from the book, from the law of God, translating to give the sense so that they understood the reading." This verse attests that the Torah was read aloud publicly to crowds in Hebrew, and also translated verbally into Aramaic for those who had returned, but had forgotten Hebrew. Centuries later as synagogues were planted in Greek-speaking lands, the Septuagint translation was largely used in the liturgy and worship. We see here the beginnings of how services were to be conducted in the Jewish Synagogue, with the focus being the reading of the Torah and the Prophets.

Some in the more independent Messianic community believe that assembling for worship services on *Shabbat* is not what the Leviticus 23 commandment directs, and that *Shabbat* is only about "rest." But if this were the case, then we would see it borne out in the actions of Yeshua and the Apostles. Yeshua the Messiah's custom was to go to the synagogue on *Shabbat*. The narrative of Luke 4:17-20 shows how He was handed a scroll of Isaiah and read it aloud publicly. A cursory reading of the Book of Acts will reveal time and time again that the Apostles, notably Paul, would always go to the local Jewish synagogue in a city and reason with the Jews—on *Shabbat*—from the Torah and the Prophets regarding who Yeshua was as the Savior of Israel. Surprisingly to many people, the post-Reformation Christian custom of going to Church on Sunday, submitting to some kind of "Sunday school" teaching, and then engaging in corporate worship and instruction, is loosely based on the practices of the First Century Jewish Synagogue.

What should we do today to fulfill the commandment to have a holy convocation in regard to Sabbath observance? It is fairly safe to say that in a community where you can assemble and fellowship at a Messianic congregation—*that you should*. The important thing that only a few non-Jewish Believers in the Messianic movement realize is that the Torah is to be kept in a community. The Torah should not be kept as though you are a hermit in a cave somewhere or out on a deserted island. The Torah is to be kept where you can be accountable to other people, and solicit their opinions—*especially the opinion of a qualified "rabbi."* The Jewish community today is centered around the local synagogue, and Jewish rabbis have the profound responsibility in instructing members of the Jewish community in how they are to function as Torah observant members of society. Interestingly enough, the Protestant Reformers used the template of the Jewish rabbi to train pastor-teachers. While "rabbi" (Heb. *rav*, רַב) is merely a Hebrew term meaning "teacher," a rabbi also functions as a spiritual mentor to his fellow Jews. A pastor-teacher likewise must be a teacher, but be responsible for the spiritual well-being of his parishioners.

The challenge, for some in the Messianic community, is that in some locations Messianic congregations are few-and-far-between. As a maturing religious movement, some people have to drive long distances to attend a Messianic congregation, that is if any one can be found. With many no longer feeling comfortable at a local "church," they are left to keep *Shabbat* in their homes with family members and close friends. Is this in violation of the commandment to make *Shabbat* a "holy convocation"? Must it always be done in some kind of assembly building? No. In fact, as many of you may not be aware, many Jewish synagogues in the First Century Diaspora met in homes. There were only synagogue buildings in cities where there were large Jewish communities. In Corinth, for example, the Believers were actually booted out of the synagogue, and instead assembled in the home of Titius Justus, who lived right next to the synagogue (Acts 18:7). In Philippi, which was administered as a Roman military colony with a high Roman patriotism, the Jews were not permitted to establish a religious assemblage and instead had to go outside the city to pray by the riverside (Acts 16:3). Keeping *Shabbat* in one's home is consistent with many examples that we see in the First Century community of faith. Oftentimes new Messianic fellowships have had to begin in the home. But this by no means discounts the value of a larger, established Messianic congregation that meets in its own "building." The command is ultimately that the Sabbath is to be a special time of assemblage for instruction, teaching, and spiritual exhortation by worshipping the Lord.

3. Work is to be done in the first six days of the week.

The purpose of the days leading up to *Shabbat* are detailed for us quite clearly in Exodus 20:9: "Six days you shall labor and do all your work." In this text, we see the two words *avad* and *melakah* employed together: "Six days shall you work [*avad*] and accomplish all your work [*melakah*]." Context clearly indicates that *avad* and *melakah* are indeed connected together and are somewhat synonymous. The Septuagint translation makes no distinction rendering *ta'avod* as the verb *erga* (ἔργα), and *melakah* is rendered by the noun *erga*. What is perhaps most interesting is that the Hebrew verb *ta'avod* (תַּעֲבֹד) appears in the Qal imperfect tense, meaning that an absolute literal translation could appear as "You work," but that the LXX translators thought of it as *erga*, appearing in the (more specific) future middle indicative tense. *Erga* could be translated into English as "you will work," and that you are involved in the work as though it is unavoidable. This is because work is a part of the human condition that each one of us must experience.

Whether we personally "like" work or not, surprisingly there is to be a Divine calling when it comes to one's work. This is realized when we examine many of the varied Jewish and Christian traditions regarding the workweek. J.H. Hertz writes, "Work during the six days of the week is as essential to man's welfare as is the rest on the seventh. No man or woman, howsoever rich, is freed from the obligation of doing some work, say the Rabbis, as idleness invariably leads to evil thoughts and evil deeds."[11] The Protestant work ethic, which largely came from the teachings of John Calvin and others, was birthed out of the belief that if one is a member of God's elect, then he will demonstrate it through faithful labors during the six days designated for work. This even led to some of the Reformers preaching that if an individual does not work during the designated time, that he or she is actually sinning! Of course, the Protestant Reformers were limited by their inability to see the validity of *Shabbat*, as opposed to the Christian Sunday,[12] but to many of them a "Sunday sabbath" was rigidly enforced, and no work of any kind was permitted. The Protestant work ethic largely

---

[11] J.H. Hertz, ed., *Pentateuch & Haftorahs* (London: Soncino Press, 1960), 297.

[12] Of course, while the principle of one-day-in-seven was believed to be valid by these Protestant Reformers and theologians, they believed that the Messiah's so-called "Sunday resurrection" validated the transfer of the Sabbath from the seventh day to the first day. The Reformers did not have access to the Jewish resources that we have today, which continually show us that the Apostles kept *Shabbat*. Nevertheless, God did great deeds through these men and women, and we would not be where we are today without them.

led to the great technological advances made in Northwestern Europe and Great Britain, which were largely not paralleled in Catholic France and Southern Europe.

In the Jewish and Christian traditions, work is really not something that is looked down upon. It is simply something that people are supposed to do. Of course in our modern context in the West, we generally have a five-day work week, with both Saturday and Sunday off. In our society this has allowed for Jewish people to worship on the Sabbath, and for Christians to go to church on Sunday. Generally, this allows for Messianic Believers to abstain from working on *Shabbat*. However, it is very easy to say that many of us have lost sight of what it means to truly "work," and what it likewise means for us to truly "rest." Many Christian pastors today have observed that we live in a "weekend culture," where one works and works, but does not take seriously a day of rest that God has prescribed. Is this occurring because the Lord is in the process of restoring the seventh-day Sabbath to all of His people, and that by keeping *Shabbat* on the right day of the week we will be able to truly experience *all of the rest that He has for us?*

Interestingly enough, while it is easy for some in the Messianic community to accuse Christians who do not even take a "Sunday sabbath" that seriously, of holding to "Greek" or "Hellenistic" ideas of "work," the modern-day concept of work really does not have that much in common with the Hellenistic idea of work. The modern concept of work is largely focused around financial theories, the stock and trade markets, and any plan for companies and individuals to make the most money during all days of the week, regardless of whether or not the stock market is closed on Saturday and Sunday. Jews and many Christians over the centuries have historically viewed work as being something that was a calling given to them by God. The Greeks, in stark contrast, viewed work as nothing less than a curse that people were to avoid at all costs. R. Paul Stevens explains the Greek view of work in his book *The Other Six Days*:

"While there was no uniformity in the ancient Greek world in its view of work, the classical period generally held work in disdain, especially the philosophers. Work was a curse, unmitigated evil; and to be out of work was a piece of singularly good fortune.

Unemployment allowed for one to participate in the political domain and to enjoy the contemplative life. The whole of society was organized so that a few could actualize the highest human potential. Not surprisingly, 80 per cent of the Greek city-states were comprised of slaves, which Aristotle defined as instruments endowed with life. Work was called 'unleisure'."[13]

When the Hebrew Scriptures were translated into Greek several centuries before Yeshua, the Jewish translators rendered Exodus 20:9 as "you will work" in the (specific) future tense. Perhaps this is because they knew that those who would be reading it did not have a high view of work. When such Greeks would accept the God of Israel as the One True God, and entered into the community of Israel, many of them would then be forced to finally "work."

It is absolutely true that we see Greeks and Romans of the First Century criticizing the Jewish people for taking a complete day off of work on the Sabbath. Such Jews were often criticized as being "lazy." But what was the context of this? Jewish people in ancient times, and largely today, are often described as being very industrious, productive, and successful. A Greek or Roman slave, or common worker, could see such people and easily criticize them as being "lazy" or "slothful" for taking off a day of rest. Do we not see the same thing even happening to us who are industrious during the workweek and then take *Shabbat* off?

One of the challenges for many in the Messianic community today is that many people, because of our modern world, must still go to work on *Shabbat*. This would have been largely unknown to the Ancient Israelites, or even the Jews of the First Century. Clearly this would be prohibited by the Torah, but difficult ethical questions are posed nonetheless. What if a husband and/or wife still has to go to work to support the family? What if someone is a business owner in an industry that requires some work to be done on *Shabbat?* What happens if someone does not work on the Sabbath, but is called in to work?

Thankfully, we live in a time when Messiah Yeshua has come and has been sacrificed for our sins. His atoning work at Golgotha (Calvary) covers any violation of God's commandments, be it

---

[13] R. Paul Stevens, *The Other Six Days* (Grand Rapids: Eerdmans, 1999), 110.

intentional or unintentional. He was the one who asked a group of Pharisees, "have you not read in the Law, that on the Sabbath the priests in the temple break the Sabbath and are innocent?" (Matthew 12:5). The priests were doing the hard, sweaty, dirty, back-breaking work of sacrificing animals, putting them on the altar to burn, and cleaning up their charred remains—among some of their responsibilities. Certainly, if the priests in the Temple were not considered violating the Sabbath for doing this work, then in our modern world, when "life happens" and you are required to work, God's grace is there to cover us. If you are in a difficult position that requires you to work on the Sabbath, please pray that God enables you to find favor with your employer, who will let you work on Sunday instead, or schedule you differently. There are always exceptions to the rule, as is continually shown in Scripture. But the existence of exceptions likewise does not mean that we should *desire to work on Shabbat*. We all go to our Father daily to ask for His provision, and should ask Him that we not have to receive that provision by violating the Sabbath day.

4. The Sabbath is to be a day of complete rest.

Repeated in the midst of the Exodus narrative, the commandment to rest on the Sabbath day is given: "You shall work six days, but on the seventh day you shall rest; *even* during plowing time and harvest you shall rest" (Exodus 34:21). Whereas in Deuteronomy 5:14, the Hebrew verb *nuach* (נוּחַ) is used for "rest," Exodus 34:21 reads with, *u'b'yom hashevi'i tishvot* (וּבַיּוֹם הַשְּׁבִיעִי תִּשְׁבֹּת), "on the seventh day you shall rest." The verb for rest in this text is *shavat* (שָׁבַת), appearing in the Qal stem (simple action, active voice), meaning "to **rest, celebrate**, with direct or indirect connection with the Sabbath" (*HALOT*).[14] The command could be understood as meaning that on the seventh day we are to *observe Shabbat*.

What a day of complete rest is, of course, is subject to a substantial amount of interpretation. When God originally gave the command to rest, He conditioned it with the requirement, "you shall cease from labor even at plowing time and harvest time" (NJPS). Anticipating that Israel would be a largely agrarian society,

---

[14] *HALOT*, 2:1407.

the Israelites were told that on the Sabbath day they were not to be out harvesting and plowing their fields, or any other agricultural activities. The principle, of course, is that ordinary work is not to be performed on *Shabbat*. In our modern age, while many of us may not have fields to harvest or crops to plant, we often do have homebound responsibilities that we like to work on during the weekend. Mowing the grass, doing yardwork, planting things in a personal garden, cleaning one's house, washing the car, and things that can clearly be done on other days are prohibited. But there are always exceptions. Certainly if there is a storm (as our family experienced when we lived with hurricanes in Central Florida, 2000-2012) and there are fallen tree limbs in one's yard that are causing serious problems, one should remove them. Weather and climate can affect things that require immediate attention. But unnecessary yardwork or housework that can be done on another day is something else.

But what would constitute "rest" from one's labors? Is God simply expecting us to spend *Shabbat* lying on our sofas taking a nap? Not surprisingly, this is exactly what many people do. In fact, some people spend most of *Shabbat* sleeping.

One of the things that we have to keep in mind, as previously discussed, is that the Sabbath is to be a holy convocation. We should not simply enter into the *Shabbat* rest by "falling asleep." We are admonished in Scripture to convene a holy assembly, worshipping God and studying His Word. It is to be a special time of intimacy between ourselves as Believers, and the Lord. In that special time we are to be consecrated, and not be doing things that we would normally do during the rest of the workweek.

Perhaps one issue that needs to be considered is that many Messianic congregations hold their services on *Erev Shabbat* or Friday evening. Those who attend these nightly services often will stay at home Saturday. If you are one of these people, what should you be doing at home? Should you be doing yardwork or housework? Or would it be better for you to simply stay in bed? Is it a sin for you to watch television or sports games on *Shabbat?* Is it a sin for you *not* to read the Bible on *Shabbat?* Sadly, these kinds of questions are often not examined from a mature perspective by some in the Messianic community. The Sabbath is to be a time of rest, but "rest" can be interpreted and applied differently among

Believers. But one thing is absolutely certain: what goes on in a person's home is that man or woman's personal business. If you criticize a person for doing things on *Shabbat* that you would personally not do, than that person should have every right to criticize you in like manner. If a Messianic Believer is doing something on *Shabbat* that you believe violates the principle of "rest," then lead by your example and demonstrate the better way in a positive tone, and not in a superior attitude that is condemning. Remember how Yeshua said that the Sabbath was made for us; we were not made for the Sabbath.

5. Fire shall not be kindled on the Sabbath.

There is probably no commandment more contested today in regard to the Sabbath than Exodus 35:3: "You shall not kindle a fire in any of your dwellings on the sabbath day." The decree, "Do not light a fire in any of your homes on the Sabbath day" (HCSB) has been a cause of an unbelievable amount of applications and opinions regarding what it actually means to "light a fire." In ancient times, lighting a fire was serious work, as a person had to go and collect wood, perhaps even cutting down a tree, and get a flint and strike and strike and strike and hope that a spark would appear that could ignite a fire. There was a challenge to keep the fire lit. The ancients did not know what we know today about the chemical process of combustion, and certainly did not have matches or lighter fluid to aid them in creating a fire. They definitely did not know about the petroleum fuels that power most of our moving vehicles—to say nothing of elements like uranium or plutonium used in nuclear power.

The Jewish Rabbis used the premise that this commandment could only be properly interpreted via application of the Oral Law, if not it would be subject to a gross amount of improper interpretations. The Orthodox Jewish *ArtScroll Chumash* gives us a good summary of how the command has been interpreted in Jewish history:

"This prohibition is indicative of the Jewish principle that the Torah can be understood only as it is interpreted by the Oral Law, which God taught to Moses, and which he transmitted to the nation. The Oral Law makes clear that only the creation of a fire and such use of it as cooking and baking are forbidden, but there is no prohibition against enjoying its light and heat. Deviant sects that denied the teachings of the Sages misinterpreted this passage to refer to *all* use of fire, so they would sit in the dark throughout the Sabbath, just as they sat in spiritual darkness all their lives."[15]

Orthodox Jewish *halachah* today demonstrates that not only is the lighting of an actual "fire" considered prohibited, but likewise turning on any kind of electric device, including a lightswitch or the ignition to a car, is considered in violation of the commandment. This is why many Orthodox Jews have automatic timers on their lights, so that they do not have to perform any work. The practice of having a "Sabbath *goy*," or a Gentile to do the work of lighting a fire on *Shabbat*, was adhered to in many Jewish communities. Adam Clarke, writing in the early Nineteenth Century, observes to this end, "The Jews understand this precept as forbidding the kindling of fire only for the purpose of doing work or dressing victuals; but to give them light and heat, they judge it lawful to light a fire on the Sabbath day, though themselves rarely kindle it—they get Christians to do this work for them."[16]

Conservative Judaism in the United States has a less rigorous interpretation of this commandment. While lighting a fire to be baking something is considered forbidden, flipping a light or electronic appliance on is not. Conservative Jews do not consider driving on *Shabbat* to be sinful, provided that one is driving to the synagogue. It is clear in the Book of Acts, for example, that the Apostles largely held to the tradition of only walking a Sabbath day's journey: "Then they returned to Jerusalem from the mount called Olivet, which is near Jerusalem, a Sabbath day's journey away" (Acts 1:12). However, they did not anticipate the modern age where now cars and other *machines* exist to transport people. The big issue is, regarding what "lighting a fire" truly is, is to what extent the evolution of technology should affect our interpretation of this passage.

The Rabbinical tradition widely concludes that cooking or baking food on the Sabbath day is prohibited. Obviously, this is why

---

[15] Nosson Scherman, ed., *ArtScroll Chumash, Stone Edition* (Brooklyn: Mesorah Publications, Ltd., 2000), 517.

[16] *Adam Clarke's Commentary on the Bible*. E-Sword 7.6.1. MS Windows 9x. Franklin, TN: Equipping Ministries Foundation, 2005.

on the day before *Shabbat* Jewish homes over the centuries would be a center of cooking and baking so food for the Sabbath would be ready. But the Rabbis did not anticipate the day of microwaves and packaged foods that one could easily just put into an oven and have prepared for a person. Cooking and baking in the context before our modern age involved much, much more than just unzipping something from a package. It involved a great amount of pre-preparation time, i.e., giving bread the time to rise, peeling potatoes and onions, letting vegetables and meat soak, and other things which modern technology has either eliminated or streamlined. Furthermore, the Rabbis of ancient times did not anticipate the creation of what may be humankind's ultimate culinary creation: the sandwich.

If there is anything that the Messianic community does not want, it is to interpret this passage in a very strict sense so as to be left cold and in the dark on *Shabbat*. The quotation above is particularly directed against the Karaites, a rebellious Jewish sect that rejects all of the Oral Torah and adheres to a very narrow minded and fundamentalist interpretation of the Tanach text only. Karaite theology is sadly prevalent in some areas of the broad Messianic movement today. But I do not think that most Messianics want to sit in the dark eating cold bread on the Sabbath. Likewise, I do not think that most Messianics want to be worried about what it means to "light a fire," either. Is the modern Orthodox perspective equally wanting? Is it really work to flip on a light, or even heat something up in a microwave or toaster oven? These are all personal value judgments that we have to make ourselves.

My personal opinion regarding this commandment is that in ancient times, it was major work to get a fire started. It was major work to keep a fire from going out. God did not want His people taking His Sabbath day going through all the motions of lighting a fire when they should be spending that same time with Him and with others in the community of faith. But today we do live in a modern age when the technological level has changed our ability to manipulate "fire." The ancients did not have the ability to strike a match and ignite a gas fireplace with the ease that we have today. The ancients did not have electricity or microwave ovens. The ancients, if they took any "vehicle" to their synagogues, had to ride donkeys (and possibly horses), as animals which would require rest;

they could not just turn the ignition to their cars. Any proper Messianic interpretation of this commandment will take into consideration the progress of technology. I will say that I do not consider it a sin to drive on the Sabbath, or even microwave leftovers from the *Shabbat* meal the night before. But if I am engaging in strenuous work on the Sabbath, which involves fire, electricity, or my car, that is probably something else. We each have the responsibility to go to the Lord and see how this commandment is to be applied in our modern world.

6. On the Sabbath, God's people are to remember that the Ancient Israelites were once slaves in Egypt.

One of the most unique commandments concerning *Shabbat* appears in the repetition of the Ten Commandments in Deuteronomy 5:15: "You shall remember that you were a slave in the land of Egypt, and the LORD your God brought you out of there by a mighty hand and by an outstretched arm; therefore the LORD your God commanded you to observe the sabbath day." Presumably, the admonition to remember the slavery in Egypt is connected to the wonderful rest that the Sabbath offers. The Ancient Israelites in bondage did not receive a Sabbath day of rest. The only "rest" any of them experienced would have been going to sleep every night with the anticipation of having to go out and work the next day for the Egyptians. Finally as Israel was constituted as a nation, people could sleep one evening out of the week and know that a laborious day of work was not ahead.

Jeffrey H. Tigay does indicate that there is some variance of opinion as to what Deuteronomy 5:15 fully means, which is worth noting. He remarks, "Commentators are divided over what this motive emphasizes. Some believe that it is the memory of the servitude, to create empathy for the servant's need to rest. Others believe it is God's redeeming them from Egypt, to remind the people of His kindness and of His authority to establish such a command."[17]

For us as Messianic Believers, how do we apply the commandment to remember that the Ancient Israelites were slaves in Egypt? Not all of us are physical descendants of the Patriarchs,

---

[17] Jeffrey H. Tigay, "Deuteronomy," in *Etz Hayim*, 1020.

and our ancestors were not all in Egypt. Through faith in Messiah Yeshua, however, we are all a part of the Commonwealth of Israel, and whether we are Jewish or non-Jewish, we all partake of the same Biblical heritage. This is why the Apostle Paul could write the Corinthians with confidence, "For I do not want you to be unaware, brethren, that our fathers were all under the cloud and all passed through the sea" (1 Corinthians 10:1). For Paul to write a mixed group of Jews and non-Jews and say that "our ancestors" (NRSV) went through the Red Sea crossing is to assert that the same spiritual heritage that a First Century Jewish Believer had, knowing that his ancestors were slaves in Egypt, is the same spiritual heritage ***any*** Believer in Yeshua has. Furthermore on an individual level, unless we have the blood atonement of Yeshua the Messiah covering our lives, we cannot be considered "free from Egypt." Before each one of us came to faith in Yeshua, we were in spiritual bondage and slavery to sin. Yeshua has freed us from these things as our Passover Lamb and atoning sacrifice.

It is important as we keep *Shabbat* to remember that in Egypt the Ancient Israelites were not able to partake of this great blessing. In many of the Sabbath liturgies that are canted in the Jewish Synagogue, as well as in many Messianic congregations, the command to remember the bondage of Egypt and the mighty deliverance of God is repeated. If we hear such liturgies, it is important to praise the Lord for His miraculous acts those many centuries ago, and the much more recent deliverance from sin that each one of us has experienced, enabling us to *truly rest*, both physically **and** spiritually, on *Shabbat*.

7. God's people are not to be concerned about their own carnal pleasures.

The Torah is not the only part of Scripture that issues admonitions concerning the Sabbath. The Prophet Isaiah explains that God's people are not supposed to be concerned about themselves on *Shabbat*. He proclaims,

"If because of the sabbath, you turn your foot from doing your *own* pleasure on My holy day, and call the Sabbath a delight, the holy *day* of the LORD honorable, and honor it, desisting from your *own* ways, from seeking your *own* pleasure and speaking *your own* word, then you will take delight in the LORD, and I will make you ride on the heights of the earth; and I will feed you *with* the heritage of Jacob your father, for the mouth of the LORD has spoken" (Isaiah 58:13-14).

What this text means and how it should be applied is subject to a large amount of debate. The Hebrew word *chefetz* (חֵפֶץ) largely means, "**delight, pleasure**," perhaps more specifically "*that in* which one takes delight, his business (late), or *matter* (very late, cf. Mish.=*thing*)" (*BDB*).[18] The English translations of this word reflect a variance of interpretations, including: "your own needs" (ATS), "your affairs" (NJPS), and "your own interests" (NRSV). When we see these things in the Biblical text, we can only wonder, "What does God mean by *my pleasures?* Is this not open to a wide variance of subjective applications?"

The most obvious application of the text here pertains to a prohibition on anything that would contradict the Sabbath commandments of not working, not lighting a fire, or doing anything that would clearly violate the admonition to rest. If, for example, one is a gourmet cook and takes great pleasure in cooking, then one should not cook on *Shabbat*. This would cause a person to work, often light some kind of fire well beyond a "minimum" usage of microwaving something or heating something up, and would take a person away from the Sabbath rest that God intended. The intent of *Shabbat* is for us as God's people to focus on Him, His Word, and what He has done for us. Things that very clearly take us away from the Lord, and cause us to focus on ourselves and what we are doing, seem to be implied by Isaiah's words.

Questions that often have to be fielded frequently come from those who are often stuck at home on *Shabbat*. As many Messianic congregations have *Erev Shabbat* services, many do not go anywhere on Saturday. What are these Messianic Believers to do? Are they required to either sleep all day, or only read the Scriptures and/or religious literature? Are they permitted to watch television and sports games, walk in their neighborhood, read books, talk to friends or loved ones on the phone, and generally take a day off? Are husbands and wives permitted to make love? Some in the Messianic movement would say a definite "no" to these things. They would say that these sorts of things would clearly violate the

---

[18] *BDB*, 343.

commandment not to partake in personal pleasures. Others in the Messianic movement would say "yes" to these things, provided that they do not take one's attention off the Lord, as God wants us to enjoy ourselves in Him. **The truth of the matter is that what a man or woman does in his or her home is that person's personal business.** Our Heavenly Father is gracious to each one of us, and we each have to realize that we are individually responsible for what we do on the Sabbath. May God bless each one of us for our desire to obey Him to the best of our ability, and allow us to respect others' privacy.

8. Conducting in business is prohibited on the Sabbath.

The last of the Biblical prohibitions regarding *Shabbat* is derived from Nehemiah 10:31: "As for the peoples of the land who bring wares or any grain on the sabbath day to sell, we will not buy from them on the sabbath or a holy day; and we will forego *the crops* the seventh year and the exaction of every debt." This text records how the Southern Kingdom exiles returned from Babylon and adapted to the new environment of trying to rebuild the Temple and largely be retrained in the commandments of the Torah. Just as there were many who taunted Nehemiah, saying that the Temple or walls surrounding Jerusalem could not be rebuilt, so were there those who had occupied the Land of Israel during the Jews' exile who did not follow the Torah. They were the *ammei ha'aretz* (עַמֵּי הָאָרֶץ), "the peoples of the land." These were not Israelites, but pagans who had occupied the Land of Israel during the exile.

These people did not know the command to rest from one's labors on the Sabbath day, and as the foundation of what would advance into Second Temple Judaism was being laid, and as the city of Jerusalem was being reconstructed and reconstituted, these people still had access to the city and could bring in their wares to sell on *Shabbat*. Civil order and police had not been established to the point of preventing this. Jews living in Jerusalem had to consciously make the choice of whether to abstain from buying on *Shabbat* or not. As selling a product was considered to be a form of work, the Judaisms of the First Century largely regarded conducting in business to be a prohibited practice on the Sabbath. While work, business, trade, and industry could be practiced the previous six days of the week, and history bears the testimony of many able Jewish businessmen and merchants, the command to separate the Sabbath day likewise is to be observed.

What we do as the Messianic community today needs to be tempered by the fact that we are not to conduct in trade on the Sabbath. We need to try as best as humanly possible to make sure that during the previous six days that we have purchased everything that we need prior to *Shabbat*, that we do not have to do any grocery shopping, and that all of our expenses are taken care of. *Shabbat* is not a time when we are permitted to go to the mall and shop of our own personal desires. *Shabbat* is a time where we are to focus on the Lord and consecrate it as a holy time.

One of the challenges, of course, is that in our society today exceptions to the rule always find themselves into our lives—and these challenges mostly are not by choice. What if somebody gets sick on *Shabbat?* Are we permitted to go to the store or pharmacy to buy medicine? Those who adhere rigidly to this principle would say "no." But the Rabbis of Judaism would all say "yes." If one is ill and needs care, then the commandment can be set aside to preserve life. This is the same reason why doctors in Israel today are allowed to work—and are *not considered to be breaking the Sabbath*. We are always going to find circumstances like somebody getting sick forced upon us that cause us to buy and sell on the Sabbath. But buying medicine to help an ill person is substantially different than going out and purchasing something that is "on sale."

Perhaps the most common form of buying and selling that has worked its way into the Messianic movement, primarily because of how common it is in American Christianity after Sunday church services, is going out to eat at a restaurant after *Shabbat* services.[19] Is it permitted for Messianics who go to a *Shabbat*

---

[19] Note that this article is not intended to discuss the application of the dietary laws in the modern world. There are some fundamentalist Messianic Believers who believe it is wrong to eat at a public restaurant that is not "approved kosher." Our ministry position is much more moderate in that we certainly believe that we are to follow the dietary laws and abstain from pork, shellfish, blood, etc., but we do not consider eating at a public restaurant, including certain fast food, to be wrong.

For a further discussion of the dietary laws, consult the *Messianic Kosher Helper* by Messianic Apologetics.

service to eat afterwards? If these *Shabbat* services are held late in the afternoon, and by the time they are over it is dark and no longer the Sabbath, then it is certainly permitted for Messianic Believers to engage in any kind of commerce they want to. But most Messianic congregations hold late morning/early afternoon services on *Shabbat*, just like many churches do on Sunday. Is it permitted for Messianic Believers to go to a restaurant to eat on the Sabbath? Perhaps a better alternative would be for Messianic congregations—which are often small and need cohesive community—to have a covered dish lunch for members of the congregation where pre-prepared food can be heated up in which all can partake.

As with all of the Sabbath prohibitions we see in Scripture, the ordinance to abstain from buying and selling ultimately must be decided by you. You must use your own judgment and discernment when life circumstances are thrust upon you that may require you to buy something on the Sabbath. Ultimately, the responsibility is on you, and is between you and the Lord.

Leading By Our Example

This concludes our analysis of the guidelines that the Bible itself offers regarding how we should celebrate the Sabbath and make it a special time between ourselves and our Heavenly Father. As it should be emphasized, we have only scratched the surface regarding what we should and should not do on *Shabbat*. There have been many debates in ancient Judaism, and there are many debates today in Orthodox and Conservative Judaism, regarding how the Sabbath is to be properly kept. These debates have spilled over into the Messianic community. It is doubtful that we will ever have a consensus of opinion relating to what we should be doing on *Shabbat*. Each congregation or fellowship of Messianic Believers is different, just like each one of us individually is different. Some will choose to follow a very strict, rigid interpretation of the Sabbath commandments, and others will choose to relatively ignore them. I personally believe that we should strive for a safe position, where we do strive to keep the Sabbath's commandments, but at the same time keep them in a modern context that respects both ancient and modern Jewish opinion.

The major challenge that exists for the Messianic community in relation to Sabbath keeping is going to be avoiding the fundamentalist trap of thinking that there is only one right way to keep the Sabbath, and those who are not following this "one right way" are not keeping *Shabbat* at all. We cannot and should not spend our time arguing and debating why "we are right" and why "everyone else is wrong." We should rather be encouraging one another through our obedience, and if an interpretation of a Sabbath commandment is truly correct, then a person should be convicted by the Holy Spirit that this is correct and he or she will adapt it. Force-feeding one's personal *halachah* on someone, however, will only cause problems. There is a substantial amount of subjectivity relating to how the Sabbath is to be properly kept, as well as issues of privacy concerning how much a local congregation or fellowship should intrude itself into the affairs of one's family. We each have an individual responsibility to obey the Lord, which exceeds the responsibility we have toward each other.

You do not need to feel condemned if you do not keep the Sabbath the way other people do. Your opinions about *Shabbat* will change over time as you keep it more and more. *Shabbat* is to be a time of joy and delight—*not a time of burdensome legalism*. But even so, *Shabbat* is to be a special time when we abstain from certain things. There are ethical and ideological decisions you have to make concerning the Sabbath day, and hopefully you have a strong relationship with God through Yeshua to help you make the right decision for yourself and your family, which will help the cohesion of the community of Believers at large. And, there are many theological issues that must be discussed as the Messianic movement continues to mature and examine Scripture in a more systematic manner. May we all make the right decisions, and be edifying to one another in everything that we do.

Being Realistic About Shabbat

That the seventh-day Sabbath or *Shabbat* is to be a holy time, sanctified unto the Lord, is clear enough from the Torah: "Observe the day of *Shabbat*, to set it apart as holy, as *ADONAI* your God ordered you to do" (Deuteronomy 5:12, CJB). It is also stated how "the seventh day is a sabbath of the LORD your God; *in it* you shall not do any work" (Deuteronomy 5:14). Frequently in much of today's Messianic movement, what is witnessed is that the seventh-day Sabbath is simply a time for Believers to attend services at their local Messianic congregation, and for various other congregational activities. While congregational activities such as corporate worship, teaching, and fellowship do provide a legitimate way for people to consciously honor *Shabbat*—many questions do arise regarding work, permissible and non-permissible activities, and most especially what to do when "life happens." Tension can arise between people inside and outside of one's local assembly, with some thinking that one type of *Shabbat* observance is too lenient and liberal, and others thinking that another type of *Shabbat* observance is too rigid and inflexible. Surely, as we evaluate Biblical instruction, some traditional interpretations, and weigh some of the realities of Twenty-First Century living—the possibility does exist for us to come to a realistic orientation of making the Sabbath a holy and blessed time.

The Sabbath is something that takes place every seven days, and when in conscious view of the people of God, is something that will naturally be distinguished from the other six working days. In fact, the Hebrew *Shabbat* (שַׁבָּת), in the plural *shabbaton* (שַׁבָּתוֹת), can actually mean "**weeks** (i.e. from one sabbath to next)" (*CHALOT*).[1] For the observant Jew, it is the Sabbath occurring every seven days, that becomes the focal point of his or her week. While he or she may have a job to go to, home responsibilities to see taken care of, and other religious activities to be involved with—the pinnacle of the week involves the arrival of *Shabbat*, and the different preparations and duties to see *Shabbat* made into a special time. Such a special time will not just involve an abstention from normal labors, but also gathering for *Shabbat* dinner with family and friends, attending synagogue services, physically resting, and most especially focusing oneself onto God and His Word. While it can be very difficult—given the complexity that many face with modern living—keeping *Shabbat* and benefitting from the refreshment that it offers, needs to be preceded in the working week with important physical and spiritual disciplines. In his book *Shabbos: The Sabbath—Its Essence and Significance*, Shimon Finkelman indicates,

"If one prepares himself spiritually in the days leading up to Shabbos, then he will reap the reward of heightened spirituality that he will experience on Shabbos; but if one enters Shabbos in a frenzy, preoccupied with his daily affairs until the last minute, is it any wonder if he senses little uplift on this most coveted of days?"[2]

***Shabbat* is hardly a time for people to show up late to a Saturday morning service, and then leave early.** *Shabbat* is to be much more, with far more than just passive effort expelled. However, given Yeshua's famed word, "The Sabbath was made to meet the needs of people, and not people to meet the requirements of the Sabbath" (Mark 2:27, NLT), it is hardly appropriate for the Sabbath to be viewed as a time of forced "unwork"—because what it is instead, is a God-ordained time of cessation.

To be sure, given the different Torah and Tanach prohibitions present for *Shabbat*—including, but not limited to: field labor (Exodus 34:21), traveling outside of one's area (Exodus 16:29-30), kindling a fire (Exodus 35:3), carrying a load (Jeremiah 17:22), and treading a winepress and loading animals (Nehemiah 13:15-18)—

---

[1] *CHALOT*, 360.

[2] Shimon Finkelman, *Shabbos: The Sabbath—Its Essence and Significance* (Brooklyn: Mesorah Publications, 1990), 86.

there are many derived applications to be considered for Twentieth and Twenty-First Century living. Beyond this, given some of the traditional applications of prohibited work in the Jewish theological tradition—most especially including the thirty-nine prohibitions based on the work employed to construct the Tabernacle (m.*Shabbat* 7:1)—more can be considered. Too much of our Messianic faith community, though, does not go into discussing prohibitions on work or commerce—because all too frequently people will start issuing excuses as to why they cannot expel that much effort to alter many of their activities.

Rather than unaddressed and unmentionable tensions continuing unabated, we need to have some honest conversation about keeping *Shabbat* as Messianic people. The seventh-day Sabbath was taken very seriously by ancient Jews, many of whom died to keep it during times of persecution—but who also recognized that there would inevitably be life issues arise that would require God's people to be flexible. Some interesting, and even esoteric views, of what takes place on the Sabbath, did arise in some branches of Judaism. At the same time, making sure that there were clearly defined categories of labor and work, has also occurred, from which we can take some guidance, and do need to be informed of.

Ancient people seeking to follow the God of Israel had to sort and reason through some of the same issues that today's Messianic people do, as they desired to make *Shabbat* a holy and sanctified day. Hopefully, in your quest to keep the Sabbath, our realistic examination of some of the key components of what ancient Jews have wrestled with, and what present Messianics can be uncertain about—can provide you with a sense of relief. Our Heavenly Father's intention is to welcome us into *Shabbat*, but we also have to make sure that we have made the preparations, and are expelling the effort, to enter into what it offers (cf. Isaiah 58:13-14).

Commandments to Which People Give Up Their Lives

Within the Torah, it is witnessed that violation of *Shabbat* did merit capital punishment: "Therefore you are to observe the sabbath, for it is holy to you. Everyone who profanes it shall surely be put to death; for whoever does any work on it, that person shall be cut off from among his people" (Exodus 31:14; cf. 35:2). While

"Whoever does any work on the day of *Shabbat* must be put to death" (Exodus 31:15, CJB) highlights how important God considers the Sabbath to be for His people, it is hardly as though every minor infraction of the Sabbath merited execution. There were not never-ending lines of Ancient Israelites being executed for violating the Sabbath. It is fairly obvious that within Ancient Israel, and certainly witnessed later in Judaism, that procedures would have to be observed by the authorities in order to convict one accused of Sabbath violation, with facts and testimonies to be evaluated. A resource like *Pentateuch & Haftorahs* by J.H. Hertz generally states,

"This extreme penalty was only to be inflicted if the culprit desecrated the Sabbath in the presence of two witnesses who had previously warned him of the punishment that awaited him."[3]

The *ArtScroll Chumash* also notes how a court needed to sentence a Sabbath violator, but also expresses the view of how those being ignorant of *Shabbat* and violating it unintentionally, were punished by God:

"*Shall be put to death...shall be cut off.* These are two different, mutually exclusive penalties. One who violates the Sabbath despite a warning from witnesses that he is committing a capital offense is liable to the death penalty imposed by the court. But one who does so intentionally, without being warned or witnessed, is punished by God with *kareis* [or, *karat*, כרת], i.e., his soul is cut off from the nation (*Rashi*)."[4]

Why the Jewish community today, even in Israel, does not execute Sabbath violators concerns factors of civil governance. In the case of high crimes in the Second Temple period, the authority to execute criminals was solely in the hands of the Romans, indicated by how the Jewish religious leaders needed Roman approval to see Yeshua executed for blasphemy (cf. John 18:31). In the case of the First Century Body of Messiah, given Yeshua's sacrifice for human sin and the capital penalties in the Torah for which no available animal sacrifice was present, Colossians 2:14 can assert, "having canceled out the certificate of debt consisting of

[3] J.H. Hertz, ed., *Pentateuch & Haftorahs* (London: Soncino, 1960), 356.

[4] Nosson Scherman, ed., et. al., *The ArtScroll Chumash, Stone Edition*, 5th ed. (Brooklyn: Mesorah Publications, 2000), 491.

decrees against us, which was hostile to us; and He has taken it out of the way, having nailed it to the cross." Yeshua's sacrifice has nullified the capital penalties of Sabbath violation, among other high crimes in the Law of Moses.[5] But, the major reason why the Jewish State of Israel today does not execute Sabbath violators, widely surrounds how the Zionist vision was not one of a principally religious state, but instead a secular one. In this case, capital punishment would widely only be used for crimes such as murder (cf. Genesis 9:6).

Jewish history includes significant examples of how many Jews died in order that they might keep the Sabbath. In the Talmud, it is asserted, "R. Simeon b. Eleazar says, 'Any religious duty for which the Israelites gave up their lives unto death in the time of the government decrees, for instance, idolatry and circumcision, is still strongly confirmed in their possession'" (b.*Shabbat* 130a).[6] Perhaps the most pronounced example of Jews dying and being slaughtered, because they kept *Shabbat*, is witnessed during the Maccabean crisis of the Second Century B.C.E.:

"Then many who were seeking righteousness and justice went down to the wilderness to dwell there, they, their sons, their wives, and their cattle, because evils pressed heavily upon them. And it was reported to the king's officers, and to the troops in Jerusalem the city of David, that men who had rejected the king's command had gone down to the hiding places in the wilderness. Many pursued them, and overtook them; they encamped opposite them and prepared for battle against them on the sabbath day. And they said to them, 'Enough of this! Come out and do what the king commands, and you will live.' But they said, 'We will not come out, nor will we do what the king commands and so profane the sabbath day.' Then the enemy hastened to attack them. But they did not answer them or hurl a stone at them or block up their hiding places, for they said, 'Let us all die in our innocence; heaven and earth testify for us that you are killing us unjustly.' So they attacked them on the sabbath, and they died, with their wives and children

---

[5] For a further discussion, consult the entry for Colossians 2:14 in *The New Testament Validates Torah*, as well as the commentary *Colossians and Philemon for the Practical Messianic*.

[6] *The Babylonian Talmud: A Translation and Commentary*.

and cattle, to the number of a thousand persons" (1 Maccabees 2:29-38).

It is recognized that these people died for the cause of righteousness, but also discussions needed to take place among religious Jews whether it was valid to defend oneself on *Shabbat*. The questions asked by the Maccabean warriors, upon learning about this tragedy, were certainly valid:

"And each said to his neighbor: 'If we all do as our brethren have done and refuse to fight with the Gentiles for our lives and for our ordinances, they will quickly destroy us from the earth.' So they made this decision that day: 'Let us fight against every man who comes to attack us on the sabbath day; let us not all die as our brethren died in their hiding places'" (1 Maccabees 2:40-41).[7]

The Jewish tradition, because of threats toward one's life, has made exceptions for "work" on *Shabbat* (discussed further).

The Maccabean crisis raised the importance of how enemies of Israel would take advantage of the seventh-day Sabbath being a time of rest for the people. But it is not the only example witnessed in Jewish history of *Shabbat* observance being made illegal for the Jewish community, or anti-Semitic acts being committed against Jews in association with their Sabbath-keeping. Samuel H. Dresner details a variety of examples from the Middle Ages, the Holocaust, but also early Twentieth Century America, for how the Sabbath has been observed with various levels of threatening, from his book *The Sabbath:*

> "During the Middle Ages the secret Jews of Spain, called the Marranos, living in fear of their lives, tried to keep the Sabbath day holy. Knowing this, the leaders of the Inquisition directed their agents to ascend to the roof of the tallest building in the winter on Sabbath days and scan the city to see if any chimney failed to emit smoke, the sign, perhaps, of a cryptic Jew; or to suddenly break into a suspected Jewish home on Friday night to learn if a festive meal were in progress or Sabbath candles had been lit, even in the cellar, as was the

---

[7] For further consideration, consult the article "The Impact of the Maccabees on First Century Judaism" by J.K. McKee, appearing in the *Messianic Winter Holiday Helper*, and "The Forgotten Past" by J.K. McKee, in the December 2014 issue of Outreach Israel News.

practice among the Marranos. Despite centuries of persecution, traces of Sabbath observance have persisted among them until our day.

"Turning to modern times, the writer Anzia Yezierska gives another example, recording a vivid memory of the New York's East Side at the turn of the century.

> "As I neared the house we lived in, I paused terror stricken. On the sidewalk stood a jumbled pile of ragged house-furnishings that looked familiar—chairs, dishes, kitchen pans. Amidst bundles of bedding and broken furniture stood my mother. Oblivious of the curious crowd, she lit the Sabbath candles and prayed over them. In a flash I understood it all. Because of the loss of my wages while I was in the hospital, we had been evicted for our unpaid rent. It was Sabbath eve. My father was in the synagogue praying and my mother, defiant of disgrace, had gone on with the ceremony of the Sabbath. All the romance of our race was in the light of those Sabbath candles. Homeless, abandoned by God and man, yet in the very desolation of the streets my mother's faith burned—a challenge to all America {excerpt from *The Golden Land*}."

"Finally, an example from the Holocaust This is a story that was...[recorded]...by a victim of the concentration camps who survived and who now lives in Israel.

"In 1943 he, his brothers and his mother were imprisoned in the ghetto of Kovno. One of the things which kept them alive was the Sabbath, which they clung to with all their strength. Each week when the Sabbath came and the lights were kindled, the songs sung and the prayers recited, new life entered the souls of the Jews. The Nazis understood the power of the Sabbath among the Jews and set out to destroy it in a typically clever way. They gave the Jews their week's supply of food on Sunday, figuring that they would surely devour the small portion of bread in the first few days of the week so they would have nothing to eat by the time the Sabbath came. But the Nazis did not reckon on the power and the piety of the Jewish woman... {proceeds to quote from *Franz Rosenzweig*}."[8]

---

[8] Samuel H. Dresner, *The Sabbath* (New York: The Burning Bush Press, 1970), pp 66-68.

Saving a Life and Defending Oneself

The Torah prescribes how "For six days work may be done, but on the seventh day you shall have a holy *day*, a sabbath of complete rest to the LORD" (Exodus 35:2a), "a holy sabbath of solemn rest" (RSV), "a day of complete rest" (ATS), "a Sabbath of total rest" (Keter Crown Bible), *qodesh Shabbat shabbaton* (קֹדֶשׁ שַׁבַּת שַׁבָּתוֹן). Given the importance of the Sabbath, *shabbaton* (שַׁבָּתוֹן) meaning "sabbath observance, sabbatism" (*BDB*),[9] for Ancient Israel and most especially Second Temple Judaism, it is hardly a surprise that various enemies have taken advantage of the Sabbath as a time to attack. Examples of the Assyrians and Babylonians, the Seleucid-Greeks, and the Romans, attacking on *Shabbat*, is witnessed throughout the ancient historical record. This specifically gave rise to discussions as to whether the need to defend oneself on *Shabbat* would be in violation of the intentions of the Fourth Commandment.

ABD goes into some detail describing how the Assyrians and the Babylonians took advantage of the Southern Kingdom's observance of the seventh day, as an ideal time to attack, because the people would widely be conditioned to a state of some form of rest:

> "Sennacherib's letter written on his Judean campaign in 701 B.C. refers to his capture of Lachish on Hezekiah's 'seventh time' (*ina 7-šu*, lit. 'in his 7th time'...)...[It has been] suggested that Hezekiah's 'seventh time' refers to the sabbath, the day when its defenders rested and the Assyrians captured Lachish. If this suggestion is correct, this cuneiform text from Sennacherib 'becomes the earliest extrabiblical reference to the Sabbath' {quoting W.H. Shea, "Sennacherib's Description of Lachish and of Its Conquest"}...It corresponds to such passages as Amos 8:4; Hos 2:11-Eng 13; and Isa 1:13 where the weekly sabbath is also depicted as a day of rest.
>
> "The publication of the Chronicles of the Babylonian Kings by Wiseman in 1956 provided the date for the capture of Jerusalem 'on the second day of the month of Adar'...i.e., March 16, 597. The day was a sabbath...Also the day for the first assault against Jerusalem on January 15, 588, is again a

---

[9] *BDB*, 992.

> sabbath, based on the synchronism of the biblical date (2 Kgs 25:1; Jer 52:5; Ezek 24:1-2) with the Babylonian records. Again the fall of Jerusalem on the 9th day of the 4th month of Zedekiah's 11th year (Jer 52:5-8) is calculated to fall on a sabbath...Based on these calculations, it appears that the military strategy of the Assyrians and Neo-Babylonians utilized the seventh-day sabbath rest of the Israelites to accomplish their military-political goals.
>
> "This strategy was again used later by the Seleucids at the beginning of the Maccabean period when Jews were attacked on the sabbath but refused to resist on this day (Josephus *Ant* 12.6.2; 1 Macc 2:33-38)."[10]

The issue of defending oneself on the Sabbath became particularly critical during the Maccabean crisis of the Second Century B.C.E. Many Jews refused to defend themselves on *Shabbat* (1 Maccabees 2:32-38), believing it to be in violation of the Torah commandment to rest. Also witnessed is the post-Biblical prohibition, "...and any man who slaughters or kills anything..." (*Jubilees* 50:12).[11] As the historian Josephus would record of those who refused to go out and fight the Seleucids, "And they refused to defend themselves on that day, because they were not willing to break in upon the honour they owed the Sabbath, even in such distresses; for our Law requires that we rest upon that day" (*Antiquities of the Jews* 12.274).[12] The sad reality is that while wanting to remain faithful to observing *Shabbat*, these Jews were slaughtered.

While the Jews who chose to die rather than defend themselves did a noble deed, the Maccabean fighters led by Mattathias recognized, "If we all do as our brothers did and do not fight against the nations for our lives and for our statutes, now quickly they will annihilate us from the land" (1 Maccabees 2:40, NETS). The Maccabees led by Judah did defend themselves when attacked on *Shabbat*. Josephus recorded, "And this rule continues among us to this day, that if there be a necessity, we may fight on Sabbath days" (*Antiquities of the Jews* 12.277).[13] *The Oxford*

---

[10] Gerald F. Hasel, "Sabbath," in *ABD*, 5:853.

[11] Wintermute, in *The Old Testament Pseudepigrapha*, Vol 2, 142.

[12] *The Works of Josephus: Complete and Unabridged*, 325.

[13] Ibid.

Dictionary of the Jewish Religion records how as a result of the Maccabean period, religious rulings were issued permitting defense of oneself:

"At the time of the Maccabean Revolt, Sabbath observance was so strict that Jewish warriors preferred to be killed rather than offer resistance on that day. In response, a ruling was promulgated saying that the preservation of life overrides the observance of the Sabbath, and the warriors were allowed to fight in their own defense (*1 Mc.* 2.40-41)."[14]

It is notably seen that when the Roman Pompey sieged Jerusalem in the First Century B.C.E., that while many Jews would defend themselves on *Shabbat*, that it was nonetheless considered unacceptable to destroy siege works:

"[A]nd had it not been our practice, from the days of our forefathers, to rest on the seventh day, this bank could never have been completed, by reason of the opposition the Jews would have made; for though our law gives us permission then to defend ourselves against those who begin to fight with us and assault us, yet does it not permit us to meddle with our enemies while they do anything else. Which thing when the Romans understood, on those days which we call Sabbaths they shot nothing at the Jews, nor came to any pitched battle with them; but raised up their earthen banks, and brought their engines into such forwardness, that they might be used on the next day" (Josephus *Antiquities of the Jews* 14.63-64)."[15]

The significance of the Jewish fighters defending themselves against the Seleucid invaders, on the Sabbath, is something that notes a major shift in approach toward Sabbath *halachah*. The influence of the Maccabean crisis, and how defending oneself might mean the suspension of Biblical commands, has been seen throughout Jewish history since. In her book *The Sabbath World: Glimpses of a Different Order of Time*, Judith Shulevitz comments from a broadly progressive, American Jewish perspective, on how the Maccabees defending themselves has had a resonating impact on Jewish observance of *Shabbat*, and other Torah instructions:

---

[14] Chaim Pearl, "Sabbath," in *The Oxford Dictionary of the Jewish Religion*, 595.

[15] *The Works of Josephus: Complete and Unabridged*, 369.

"Any American with a multicultural upbringing will recognize the outlines of the story, told every year at Hanukkah. In 167 B.C.E., Antiochus IV, a Syrian-born but Greek-educated king whose empire included Judea, decided to force the Jews to become more like the Greeks. This king called himself Antiochus Epiphanes (Antiochus the Manifest, meaning that he represented a divine emanation), but he was known to the people as Antiochus Epimanes (Antiochus the Mad). He was the first to introduce religious persecution to the region. Previous rulers had treated their subjects as sources of tax revenue; they had used force to exact their tributes, but they had not required conversion. Antiochus IV, however, had lived in Rome, and had seen Rome impose the Roman civic religion on its citizens. He had watched the Roman senators quash the local Dionysian bacchanalian cults, with their drunkenness and their fertility rites, and persecute the Epicurean philosophers, who preached a hedonistic doctrine that filled the young with subversive ideas. Antiochus regarded Judaism as an unholy combination of both cult and philosophy. Like members of a cult, Jews met at night, took loyalty oaths (the Shema, which pledged allegiance to one God), and initiated new members through circumcision; like philosophers, they taught repugnant ideas out of books.

"And so, the two books of Maccabees recount, Antiochus decided to 'Hellenize' the Jews. He looted the Temple and garrisoned soldiers in Jerusalem. He put an idolatrous statue in the Temple...erected his own altars, and ordered the Jews to start sacrificing pigs on them. He forbade them to circumcise their sons or keep the Sabbath...Women who had their babies circumcised in secret were killed, and the babies were hung from their necks. Their husbands were killed as well, and so were the men who performed the circumcision. Anyone who refused to eat non-kosher food was killed.

"Many of Jerusalem's urbane, partially Hellenized Jews did as Antiochus ordered, but the Jews of the countryside did not. Instead, they rebelled. Their leader was a priest named Mattathias, in a village called Modein. First Mattathias ran a spear through a Jew who agreed to sacrifice a pig on one of Antiochus's altars, then he said, 'Whoever is zealous of the law, and maintaineth the covenant, let him follow me' [1 Maccabees 2:27]. Mattathias had many sons, and they followed him into the desert. One of them was named Judah Maccabeus, and the rebels became known as the Maccabees. They took to the mountains and, improbably, drove the king and his soldiers out of the land.

"Before that moment, however, retold every Hanukkah, came another that is decidedly not celebrated today. A large band of soldiers came down from Jerusalem to where a group of Jews identified only as the Pious Ones had shut themselves up in caves...When the Sabbath came, the soldiers lined up in front of the caves in a battle formation and shouted, 'Come forth, and do according to the commandment of the king, and ye shall live! [1 Maccabees 2:33]' The[se Jews] shouted back, 'We will not come forth, neither will we do the king's commandment, to profane the Sabbath day! [1 Maccabees 2:34]'

"When the soldiers advanced, the Jews made no effort to block the entrances to the caves. Instead, they said to one another, 'Let us all die in our innocence: heaven and earth shall testify for us, that ye put us to death wrongfully [1 Maccabees 2:37].' The tale ends like this: 'So they rose up against them in battle on the Sabbath, and they slew them, with their wives and children, and their cattle, to the number of a thousand people' [1 Maccabees 2:38].

"When Mattathias learned of the massacre, he quickly changed the laws of the Sabbath to permit self-defense, a rule that stands today, even in the strictest of Jewish circles. The rule is called *pikuach nefesh*, or 'saving a life.' The Sabbath laws *must* the flouted if keeping them puts a life or the well-being of the community in danger—a principle that, for instance, allowed Senator Joseph Liberman, a Sabbath-observant Orthodox Jew, to run for president of the United States. As he pointed out, he would have no qualms about violating Sabbath restrictions to respond to an attack or anything else that threatened the nation.

"The story of the Maccabees and *pikuach nefesh* is sometimes told to show that the Jews understood full well that, as Christ put it, 'the Sabbath was made for man, not man for the Sabbath.' The truth, however, is that the Maccabees' reform was controversial at the time...."[16]

---

[16] Judith Shulevitz, *The Sabbath World: Glimpses of a Different Order of Time* (New York: Random House, 2010), pp 77-79.

The major Rabbinic discussion on whether or not it was permissible to transgress Sabbath command in order to defend oneself, is seen in the Talmud, where it was concluded that the Sabbath was given to people, not people being given over to the Sabbath:

"R. Yosé b. R. Judah says, '"Only you shall keep my Sabbaths" (Exo. 31:13) — might one suppose that this is under all circumstances? Scripture says, "...only...," meaning, there can be exceptions.' R. Jonathan b. Joseph says, '"For it is holy to you" — it is given into your hands, you are not committed into its hands'" (b.*Yoma* 85b).[17]

Because of the importance of Jewish *halachah*—even among the most strictly Orthodox down to this day—deciding that it was acceptable for people to defend themselves on *Shabbat* has resulted in an entire array of what would be acceptable suspensions of Torah commandments, for the preservation of one's life, being witnessed in the Rabbinic tradition. The specific principle that has emerged in mainstream Jewish thought is designated by the term *pikkuach nefesh* (פִּקּוּחַ נֶפֶשׁ).[18] As is summarized in *The New Encyclopedia of Judaism*,

> "[This is the] Hebrew term for denoting the paramount obligation to ignore most religious laws when someone's life is in danger. 'You shall not stand idly by the blood of your neighbor' (Lev. 19:16) is one traditional source for this rule; another, citing Leviticus 18:5, is the rabbinic view that God's commandments are intended for man to 'live by them' and not die through their observance (*Yoma* 85b). The *pikku'aḥ nefesh* law takes account of numerous emergency situations, especially those calling for 'work' normally prohibited on the Sabbath and Jewish festivals, since 'consideration for human life' takes precedence over the Sabbath laws (*Yoma* 85a; *Shab.* 132a). In practice, holy day regulations are set aside when a sick person needs medical attention or anyone's health may be imperiled. Expectant mothers or those falling ill should be driven to a hospital; the use of a telephone is permitted; the duty to fast on

---

[17] *The Babylonian Talmud: A Translation and Commentary.*

[18] The Hebrew term *piqquach* (פִּיקּוּחַ) is Talmudic in origin, originally relating to "*removing debris...a person from under debris is,* in gen. *saving an endangered life*" (*Jastrow*, 1169).

> the DAY OF ATONEMENT is waived; doctors and nurses must attend to their patients; and even forbidden food may be consumed if it will save a life. The law of *pikku'aḥ nefesh* does not apply, however, in cases involving three cardinal prohibitions—idolatry, murder, and sexual crimes. Here, a Jew must accept martyrdom rather than transgress these commandments (*Sanh.* 74a-b)."[19]

Some of the major Rabbinic discussion on what would be permissible to violate ritual *Shabbat* adherence, in order to save a person's life, surround what it would take to rescue someone who had a building fall on himself (m.*Yoma* 8:6).[20] The Talmudic discussion on this extrapolates a number of key examples of what it would mean to help save a person's life on the Sabbath, providing some useful guidelines which have been consulted in the Jewish theological tradition ever since:

> "'And any matter of doubt as to danger to life overrides the prohibitions of the Sabbath.' *Why was it necessary to go on and say further,* And any matter of doubt as to danger to life overrides the prohibitions of the Sabbath? Said R. Judah said Rab, 'Not only of a doubt concerning danger to human life on this Sabbath did they speak, but even of a doubt concerning danger to human life on some other Sabbath later on.' *What would be an illustration? If the physicians made an estimate that the person would face a crisis of eight days, the first of which coincides with the Sabbath, what might you have supposed? Hold up until the night, so that on the man's account two successive Sabbaths should not have to be desecrated? So we are informed that that is not the case. So too it has been taught on Tannaite authority:* They heat water for a sick person on the Sabbath, whether to give it to him to

---

[19] "Pikku'aḥ Nefesh," in *The New Encyclopedia of Judaism*, 606.

[20] "Further did R. Mattiah b. Harash say, 'Who who has a pain in his throat—they drop medicine into his mouth on the Sabbath, because it is a matter of doubt as to danger to life. And any matter of doubt as to danger to life overrides the prohibitions of the Sabbath.' He upon whom a building fell down—it is a matter of doubt whether or not he is there, it is a matter of doubt whether [if he is there], he is alive or dead, it is a matter of doubt whether [if he is there and alive] he is a gentile or an Israelite—they clear away the ruin from above him. [If] they found him alive, they remove the [remaining] ruins from above him. But if they found him dead, they leave him be [until after the Sabbath]" (m.*Yoma* 8:6; Neusner, *Mishnah*, 278).

drink or to heal him with it. And they do not say, 'Wait on him, perhaps he'll live [without it].' But a matter of doubt concerning him overrides [the prohibitions of] the Sabbath. And the doubt need not be about this Sabbath, but it may be about another Sabbath [T. Shab. 15:16A-D], because any matter of doubt as to danger to life overrides the prohibitions of the Sabbath. And not only of a doubt concerning danger to human life on this Sabbath did they speak, but even of a doubt concerning danger to human life on some other Sabbath later on. And they do not say, Let the matters be done by gentiles or children, but they should be done by adult Israelites. And they do not say, 'Let these matters be done by the testimony of women, by Samaritans.' But they join the opinion of Israelites with them [to decide to save a life by violating the Sabbath] [T. Shab. 15:15F-H].

"*Our rabbis have taught on Tannaite authority:* They remove debris for one whose life is in doubt on the Sabbath. And the one who is prompt in the matter, lo, this one is to be praised. And it is not necessary to get permission from a court. How so? [If] one saw a child fall into the ocean and cannot climb up, or [if] his ship is sinking in the sea, and he cannot climb up, he spreads a net and pulls him out of there. And it is not necessary to get permission from a court [T. Shab. 15:11]. *And that is the case even though he catches fish in the net.* If he saw a child fall into a well, he breaks loose a segment of the wall around the wall and pulls him up. And the one who is prompt in the matter, lo, this one is to be praised. And it is not necessary to get permission from a court. *And that is the case, even though he turns out to make stairs.* If he saw that a door was closing on a child, he may break it down so as to get the child out. And the one who is prompt in the matter, lo, this one is to be praised. And it is not necessary to get permission from a court. *And that is the case, even though he thereby is deliberately making chips of wood.* People put out or isolate a fire on the Sabbath And the one who is prompt in the matter, lo, this one is to be praised. And it is not necessary to get permission from a court. *And that is so, even though he thereby puts out the fire. And these several cases had to be articulated. For had we heard the case concerning the sea, we might have supposed that it is permitted to rescue the child with a net, since in the interim the child might be swept away in the water, but that does not apply to the case of the child's falling into a pit, since once there,it stays there, so one might*

> *have supposed that he might not save the child without permission of the court. So it was necessary to specify that case as well. And if we had been informed only of the case of the pit, one might have supposed that in that case there is no need to get the court's permission since the child is frightened, but in the case of the door's closing on it, one might sit outside and keep the child occupied by making a noise with nuts. It was therefore necessary to specify that case in so many words.* With reference to the statement, people put out or isolate a fire on the Sabbath: why specify both 'put out' and 'isolate'? *Even if it was to the benefit of some other court [one may do so].*
>
> "Said R. Joseph said R. Judah said Samuel, 'In matters having to do with danger to life, they are not guided by the condition of the majority.' *How am I to imagine the case that is contemplated here? If I should say that there are nine Israelites and one Samaritan among them, then a majority is made up of Israelites. If it is half and half, then a matter of doubt is resolved in a lenient fashion [and there is no issue but that life is to be saved]. So it must refer to a case in which there are nine Samaritans and a single Israelite. But that too is self-evident! For you have a stationary mass, and wherever we have a stationary mass, it is regarded as a situation in which one half comprises one classification, the other half the other. No, the ruling still is necessary to cover a case in which someone has gone off to another courtyard [where he became buried in debris]. What might you have supposed? Whoever has gone off has gone off from the majority, and in this case that would then be made up of outsiders. So we are informed:* In matters having to do with danger to life, they are not guided by the condition of the majority" (b.*Yoma* 84b).[21]

In affording the Rabbinic tradition a consultative authority,[22] today's Messianic Believers should recognize a widescale Jewish acknowledgement that it is proper for a concern to save another's life, to override Sabbath ritual. For example, if one were praying on *Shabbat*, and his neighbor's house catches on fire—then by all

---

[21] *The Babylonian Talmud: A Translation and Commentary.*

[22] The issue of considering the Pharisees as having a consultative authority for matters of Torah halachah, is discussed in the exegesis paper on Matthew 23:2-3, "Who Sits in the Seat of Moses?" by J.K. McKee, appearing in the *Messianic Torah Helper.*

means should the neighbors be saved and the house on fire should be put out! *People should not be left alone to burn to death.* The kinds of examples listed above provide a framework for legitimate applications of the principle of *pikkuach nefesh* to be realized.

In modern Israel, where the Torah and the Rabbinic tradition are recognized as playing an important part in the country's civil law, businesses and public transportation may cease operation on *Shabbat*, for much of the population. Yet, the police, fire department, hospitals, and military are all working. They are working because they provide security, lest any outside enemy take advantage of a population that is largely at rest. *They are not considered in violation of* Shabbat *for performing this kind of work.*

And if this is true of people in modern Israel, it is also true of Jews in these same sorts of professions in the Diaspora—and of anyone who has to work on the Sabbath in order to provide safety and security for others.

Eclectic and Esoteric Views of *Shabbat*

While ancient Jewish literature is certainly filled with discussions on how those keeping *Shabbat* are to make it a holy and significant time, one will also be prone to encounter what can be considered eclectic and esoteric views. Genesis 2:2, for example, says, "By the seventh day God completed His work which He had done, and He rested on the seventh day from all His work which He had done." Here, the verb *shavat* (שָׁבַת), appearing in the Qal stem (simple action, active voice), would involve "*desist* from labour, *rest*" (*BDB*).[23] We know that when God's acts of creating the universe were completed, that He ceased from this work, and that from this rest the need for human beings to rest derives its significance. To what degree God might "keep *Shabbat*," however, is one that readers should not speculate about—as Divine rest far eclipses whatever human rest can ever or may ever involve. This did not, however, stop some in the Second Temple period from speculating. *Jubilees* 2:18, 30 draws the conclusion that God and His angels keep the Sabbath, and they in fact kept the Sabbath long before any human beings did:

---

[23] *BDB*, 991.

"And he told us—all of the angels of the presence and all of the angels of the sanctification, these two great kinds—that we might keep the sabbath with him in heaven and on earth...On this day we kept the sabbath in heaven before it was made known to any human to keep the sabbath thereon upon the earth."[24]

The view that God and His angels kept the Sabbath, seems eclectic. A more esoteric perspective is witnessed in the multiple "The Songs of the Sabbath Sacrifice" appearing in the Dead Sea Scrolls (4QShirShabb).[25] This is a liturgy describing a Heavenly priesthood of angels serving God in the sanctuary on *Shabbat.* While it is clear enough that there are angels surrounding God in Heaven, the comparison and contrast of human to angelic worship—as though it were something for people to focus their attention upon during their *Shabbat* prayers and worship—is esoteric. The following excerpt states,

"...wonderfully to praise Your glory among the wise divine beings, extolling Your kingdom among the utterly h[oly]. They are honored in all the camps of the godlike beings and feared by those who direct human affairs, won[drous] beyond other divine beings and humans alike. They tell of His royal splendour as they truly know it, and exalt [His glory in all] the heavens of His rule. [They sing] wonderful psalms according to [their insight] throughout the highest heaven, and declare [the surpassing] glory of the King of the godlike beings in the stations of their habitation. [...] How shall we be reckoned among them? As what our priesthood in their habitations? [How shall our holi]ness [compare with their utter] holiness? [What] is the praise of our mortal tongue alongside their div[ine] knowledge? [...]."[26]

When God's people worship Him on Earth today, they do join in company with the angels and the saints in Heaven (Hebrews 12:22-23). It is also true that those of the Colossian assembly were warned about "delighting in self-abasement and the worship of the angels" (Colossians 2:18), which has been explained as either those in error directly worshipping angels *or* trying to pierce the extra-

---

[24] Wintermute, in *The Old Testament Pseudepigrapha*, Vol 2, pp 58, 59.

[25] Wise, Abegg, and Cook, 365-377; Geza Vermes, trans., *The Complete Dead Sea Scrolls in English* (London: Penguin Books, 1997), pp 321-330.

[26] Wise, Abegg, and Cook, pp 367-368.

dimensional barrier into Heaven to *really join in* to the Heavenly worship.[27] These are activities which are **off limits.**

It would also go too far so as to suggest that the existence of the universe depends on Israel and the Jewish people keeping the Sabbath, as expressed by Finkelman in his book *Shabbos,*[28] widely reflecting an Orthodox Jewish approach. While intending to highlight the importance of the weekly *Shabbat*, the Talmudic statements implying that those who keep *Shabbat* have their idolatry forgiven of them, also goes unacceptably off the map:

"Said R. Hiyya bar Abba said R. Yohanan, 'Whoever keeps the Sabbath in accord with its rule, even if he worships an idol like the generation of Enosh, do they forgive: "Blessed is Enosh who does this...who keeps the Sabbath from profaning it" (Isa. 56:2) — read the letters that yield "profaning it" as though they bore vowels to yield 'being forgiven'" (b.*Shabbat* 118b).[29]

While the importance of *Shabbat* is rightfully lauded throughout the broad selections of ancient Jewish literature—and more often than not discussions will involve what people should and should not do on the Sabbath—caution does need to be exhibited with views going beyond edification of one's fellow and community by observing its rest.

Similarities and Differences in Sabbath *Halachah*

While significant traditions such as lighting *Shabbat* candles, having an *Erev Shabbat* dinner, attending *Shabbat* services at synagogue, or *Havdallah* are present within Judaism—and also the Messianic community—a huge amount of attention regarding traditional Sabbath observance surrounds stipulations of prohibiting work or labor, and then from this permitted and prohibited activities. Certain types of work are prohibited in Tanach Scripture, notably agricultural labor (Exodus 34:21) and commercial trade (Nehemiah 13:15-22). Some of the first major lists of activities where Jewish (sectarian) authorities determined permitted and prohibited activities for the Sabbath are found in the

---

[27] Consult the relevant sections of the commentary *Colossians and Philemon for the Practical Messianic.*

[28] Finkelman, pp 2, 5, 55.

[29] *The Babylonian Talmud: A Translation and Commentary.*

Pseudepigrapha (*Jubilees* 2:29-30; 50:6-13) and Dead Sea Scrolls (CD 10.14-11.18). The major thirty-nine Rabbinic prohibitions are derived from the activities of Exodus 35 in constructing the Tabernacle (m.*Shabbat* 7:1-2), the applications of which have been widely expanded. While the Rabbinic tradition includes many legitimate and worthwhile points to consider, it has also been considered to be burdensome as well. The *Dictionary of Judaism in the Biblical Period* observes,

"Scripture provides only a limited description of Sabbath observance, for instance, forbidding agricultural labor even at the time of plowing or the harvest (Exod. 34:21), prohibiting trade on that day (Amos 8:5), and forbidding even discussion of one's business (Isa. 58:13). Within rabbinic Judaism, through analogy and extension of biblical prohibitions, the list of prohibited activities, as well as the description of expected or required behaviors, grew increasingly detailed. The result was a system that, in the rabbis' own description, hung like a mountain from a strand of hair, containing an inordinate number of rules, based on a small biblical foundation (M. Ḥagigah 1:8)."[30]The Qumran community was a place where observance of the Sabbath was enforced very strictly. It was permitted for one to only walk 1,000 cubits (CD 10.21) or around 500 yards, it was prohibited to wear perfume (CD 11.9-10), prohibited to lift a stone or dust (CD 11.10-11), prohibited to aid an animal in giving birth (CD 11.13) or to help an animal out that had fallen into a pit (CD 11.13-15).

Admittedly, though, the more common Sabbath *halachah* of the Pharisees was not as restrictive as that at Qumran. Still, one has to recognize the wide number of life areas that Jewish religious law from the broad Second Temple period would try to regulate. Some would prohibit sexual intercourse between husband and wife on the Sabbath (*Jubilees* 50:8), whereas others were seemingly more permissible about it (b.*Bava Qama* 82a; b.*Ketuvot* 62b). A Sabbath day's journey was more customarily 2,000 cubits, around 1,000 yards (m.*Eruvim* 4:3; 5:7; b.*Eruvim* 51a), than the Essenes' 1,000 cubits. While the Qumran community actually thought "Any living human who falls into a body of water or a cistern shall not be

---

[30] "Sabbath," in *Dictionary of Judaism in the Biblical Period*, 539.

helped out with ladder rope, or other instrument" (CD 11.16-17),[31] it stands to reason that many Jews would have not left someone in a well on the Sabbath day.

Broadly speaking for the Second Temple era, *EDB* describes how two major sets of Rabbinic tradition emerged. "In the intertestimental period, two rabbinic traditions developed concerning the sabbath. One maintained a strict sabbath observance, with an emphasis on the rules of the sabbath, while the other emphasized the concept of internal, spiritual rest" (*EDB*).[32] The Essenes or the Qumran community are regarded as being strict in most *halachah* (CD 13.1-27). To be fair to the Essenes, though, the historian Josephus would detail how the justice they would administer was not unfair, as proper procedures were observed. Describing the importance of their Sabbath observance, he recorded,

> "But in the judgments they exercise they are most accurate and just, nor do they pass sentence by the votes of a court that is fewer than a hundred. And as to what is once determined by that number, it is unalterable. What they most of all honour, after God himself, is the name of their legislator [Moses]; whom, if anyone blaspheme, he is punished capitally. They also think it a good thing to obey their elders, and the majority. Accordingly, if ten of them are sitting together, no one of them will speak while the other nine are against it. They also avoid spitting in the midst of them, or on the right side. Moreover, they are stricter than any other of the Jews in resting from their labours on the seventh day; for they not only get their food ready the day before, that they may not be obliged to kindle a fire on that day, but they will not move any vessel out of its place, nor go to stool thereon. Nay, on other days they dig a small pit, a foot deep, with a paddle (which kind of hatchet is given to them when they are first admitted among them;) and covering themselves around with their garment, that they may not affront the divine rays of light, they ease themselves into that pit, after which they put the earth that was dug out again into the pit; and even this they do only in the more lonely places, which they choose out for this purpose; and although

[31] Wise, Abegg, and Cook, 69.

[32] Ann Coble, "Sabbath," in *EDB*, 1146.

> this easement of the body be natural, yet it is a rule with them to wash themselves after it, as if it were a defilement to them" (*Wars of the Jews* 2.145-149).[33]

The Mishnah presents how in matters of Sabbath application, the Pharisaical school of Hillel, in which a figure like Paul had been trained (Acts 22:3), was much more permissible than the school of Shammai:

> "The House of Shammai say, 'They do not [on Friday afternoon] soak ink, dyestuffs, or vetches, unless there is sufficient time for them to be [fully] soaked while it is still day.' And the House of Hillel permit. The House of Shammai say, 'They do not put bundles of [wet] flax into the oven, unless there is time for them to steam off while it is still day. And [they do not put] wool into the cauldron, unless there is sufficient time for it to absorb the color [while it is still day]. And the House of Hillel permit. The House of Shammai say, 'They do not spread out nets for wild beasts, fowl, or fish, unless there is sufficient time for them to be caught while it is still day.' And the House of Hillel permit" (m.*Shabbat* 1:5-6ff).[34]

The importance of recognizing how there were differences of perspective, disagreements, and even some tensions between sects of Second Temple Judaism—such as the *halachah* of the Essenes versus the Pharisees, or sects of the Pharisees like the Shammaites versus the Hillelites—is key for recognizing the debates that would emerge in the Gospels between Yeshua of Nazareth, and various Jewish leaders. All four Gospels record various encounters between the Messiah, and various Jewish religious leaders, on *Shabbat*—and will also present some points of contention between Yeshua and His contemporaries. While some Christians have used these points of contention as a means to conclude that the Messiah abolished the seventh-day Sabbath, other Christians have seen Yeshua's discussions about Sabbath application to be well within the Jewish, and even the Pharisaic, norms of His time. Perhaps in some occasions Yeshua took the more permissive options of the day for Sabbath observance, and took them a few steps further. Yet, it is

---

[33] *The Works of Josephus: Complete and Unabridged*, pp 606-607.

[34] Neusner, *Mishnah*, 180.

becoming more and more clear to examiners, how one would be hard pressed to say that Yeshua bore an intention to expressly violate the Torah Sabbath commandments. The summary offered by *IDBSup*, draws the main conclusion that it was the authority that Yeshua stated He had, which was the main point of contention over His Sabbath observance:

> "The NT records many disputes between Jesus and the Pharisees over proper sabbath-keeping...On sabbaths Jesus' disciples plucked ears of grain without being in mortal danger, and Jesus continually healed people who were not mortally ill. These acts violated Pharisaic norms. In the Synoptic and Johannine traditions Jesus often called attention to the exceptions to sabbath-keeping which the Pharisees themselves allowed. For example, the sabbath could be 'broken' by priests making sabbath or Passover offerings (cf. Matt. 12:5), people in mortal danger (such as David—Mark 2:25-26), people aiding others in mortal danger (cf. Mark 3:4), people aiding animals (cf. Matt. 12:11; Luke 13:15; 14:5), and people circumcising a child on the eighth day (cf. John 7:22). The Pharisees also believed that God did not cease work on the sabbath. He continued to give life and to judge the dead (cf. John 5:17). Having noted such exceptions Jesus often went on to apply a traditional form of rabbinic logic: If you allow work in such lesser matters, how much more ought you to allow my work in these greater matters (Matt. 12:5-6, 11-12; Luke 13:15-16; John 7:22-23). Jesus apparently saw his healings as fulfillments of the redemptive purpose of the law. Despite the traditional form of the argument, Jesus' evaluation of the 'lesser' and the 'greater' seemed to be based on an altogether untraditional assertion of personal authority, which provoked the Pharisees' anger."[35]

The direction to observe the seventh-day Sabbath or *Shabbat* is the Fourth of the Ten Commandments (Exodus 20:8; Deuteronomy 5:12). Variance over how to interpret and apply the Biblical instructions on how to best observe the Sabbath, and even how to interpret and apply some traditional stipulations as witnessed in

---

[35] B.E. Shafer, "Sabbath," in Keith Crim, ed., *Interpreter's Dictionary of the Bible: Supplementary Volume* (Nashville: Abingdon, 1976), 760.

Second Temple Judaism, have been witnessed throughout Jewish history.

Lighting a Fire

One of the most poignant of the Torah *Shabbat* prohibitions, which has understandably seen some important discussions, and variance throughout Judaism, is Exodus 35:3: "You shall not kindle a fire in any of your dwellings on the sabbath day." The verb *ba'ar* (בָּעַר) appears in the Piel stem (intensive action, active voice), and mainly means either "*kindle*" or "*burn*" (*BDB*),[36] with a possible application involving "**maintain a fire**" (*CHALOT*).[37] The clause *lo-teva'aru eish* (לֹא־תְבַעֲרוּ אֵשׁ) is often rendered as "you shall kindle no fire" (RSV), "Do not light a fire" (NIV), or even "You are not to let fire burn" (Fox).[38] While various Jewish religious authorities have taken this direction as being a universal prohibition on not just combustible fire, but also a widescale moratorium on using most electrical devices today, a more targeted application is witnessed in the thoughts of Robert Alter. He makes the following observations in his *Five Books of Moses* translation[39]:

"This prohibition is a new specification. The lighting of fires might be well associated with the 'tasks' involved in constructing the Tabernacle because fire would have been required for all the metalwork, and in one Ugaritic text, fire is burned six days in order to erect a sanctuary for Baal. But the kindling of fire—as against merely making use of fire that has been set accidentally—is clearly a primary labor of civilization, as the Prometheus myth suggests, a kind of inauguration of technology, and so it is understandable that a special prohibition on it on the sabbath should be spelled out."[40]

With these thoughts, lighting or igniting a fire is to be taken more in the direction of fire to be used for some kind of industrial

---

[36] *BDB*, 128.

[37] *CHALOT*, 44.

[38] Everett Fox, trans., *The Five Books of Moses* (New York: Schocken Books, 1995), 463.

[39] Alter has rendered Exodus 35:3 along relatively customary lines: "You shall not kindle a fire in all your dwelling places on the sabbath day."

[40] Robert Alter, trans., *The Five Books of Moses* (New York and London: W.W. Norton, 2004), 514.

purpose, as it is indeed preceded by a repetition of how work is to be prohibited on *Shabbat* (Exodus 35:2).

The Ancient Israelites in a much more temperate Near East may not have had that many options to them to light a fire on *Shabbat*. Of course, some questions about lighting a fire must have been raised by Jews living in Central or Eastern Europe during a frosty winter. But, it is in the modern West with its electrical conveniences, and the automobile in particular, where the most amount of questions and debates reside. Debates have specifically emerged among Orthodox Jews, and Conservative and Reform Jews, the two latter groups being far more accommodating as to what it means to "light a fire." While this will involve wondering whether the usage of electrical devices such as light switches, coffee makers, and refrigerators on *Shabbat* violates Exodus 35:2—it most especially involves the issue of whether or not it is permitted for Jews to drive their cars to synagogue services on *Shabbat*. *EJ* offers the basic summary:

> "Modern inventions have produced a host of new questions regarding Sabbath observance. Orthodox Judaism forbids travel by automobile on the Sabbath, Reform Judaism permits it. Conservative Judaism has differing views on this question, but generally permits travel by automobile on the Sabbath solely for the purpose of attending synagogue. The basic legal question regarding the switching on of electric lights is whether the noncombustive type of burning produced by electricity falls under the prohibition of making a fire or any of the other [traditional] prohibitions...Orthodox Jews refrain from the use of electrical appliances on the Sabbath, with the exception of the refrigerator, which may be open and closed on the grounds that any electrical current produced in the process is incidental and without express intention. It has, however, become the practice for observant Jews to use electrical appliances on the Sabbath which are operated by time switches set before the Sabbath. In Israel, on religious kibbutzim, the same procedure is used to milk the cows on the Sabbath. Israel also has local bylaws forbidding certain activities on the Sabbath. There is, however, no comprehensive law covering the whole country. Thus, whereas the public transport does not operate on the Sabbath in Jerusalem and in Tel Aviv, it does in Haifa. Except for specifically non-Jewish sections of the

country, the Sabbath is the official day of rest on which all business and stores must close."[41]

In his book *Kosher Living: It's More Than Just the Food,* Conservative Rabbi Ron Isaacs answers the question, "Is it kosher to use electricity on Shabbat?":

"Many traditional Jews consider electricity to be a form of fire, and Jewish law prohibits making a fire on the Sabbath. Those who do not use electricity do not turn on a radio or television or use any electrical appliances on the Sabbath. Some authorities who doubt whether electricity can truly be labeled fire explain the ban on electricity as a protective measure, to safeguard against other violation that might stem from permitting the use of electrical appliances. More liberal Jews generally will use electricity on the Sabbath."[42]

Much of how Exodus 35:3 is approached may concern the differences in lighting a fire for ancient people, and how technology has changed lighting a fire, even in the form of striking a match. The *JPS Guide to Jewish Traditions* by Ronald L. Eisenberg addresses how one of the main reasons why driving on *Shabbat,* to synagogue, became permissible in Conservative Judaism, is how the Jewish community in America became spread out to more suburban areas:

> "The Rabbis interpreted the verse prohibiting the gathering of manna on the seventh day (Exod. 16:29) as forbidding one from journeying on the Sabbath. Unlike the Karaites, who took the verse 'Let no person go out of his place on the seventh day' literally and did not allow anyone to leave home on the Sabbath, the Rabbis did not restrict movement within one's home town. However, they prohibited Jews from walking more than 2,000 cubits (approximately 1/2 mile)

---

[41] Louis Jacobs, "Sabbath: Laws and Customs of the Sabbath," in Encyclopaedia Judaica. MS Windows 9x. Brooklyn: Judaica Multimedia (Israel) Ltd, 1997.

Judith Shulevitz, *The Sabbath World: Glimpses of a Different Order of Time* (New York: Random House, 2010), pp 44-46 for some of the main features of Sabbath keeping in modern Israel, in particular in Jerusalem, as well as some of the controversy that it has stirred.

[42] Ron Isaacs, *Kosher Living: It's More Than Just the Food* (San Francisco: Jossey-Bass, 2005), 193.

> beyond the town boundaries on the Sabbath, 'because traveling interrupts the rest of both man and beast' [Hertz, 277]...
>
> "Orthodox rabbis forbid driving an automobile on the Sabbath, based on the fact that it involves turning on the ignition, which in turn ignites sparks—an act that violates the Torah law against making a fire on the Sabbath (Exod. 35:3). Conservative rabbis generally permit Jews to drive on the Sabbath, but only to synagogue. This ruling was made in response to the migration of Jews to the suburbs, where most no longer live within walking distance of a synagogue. Continuing to forbid driving on the Sabbath would have forced many congregants to remain at home or to pursue nonreligious activities. Fearing an erosion of Jewish identity if synagogue attendance dropped precipitously, these rabbis permitted driving as the lesser of two evils. Orthodox rabbis denounced this decision, arguing that Conservative rabbis should instead encourage their congregants to live within walking distance of their synagogues.
>
> "In Israel, public transport does not operate on the Sabbath in Jerusalem and Tel Aviv, but it does run in Haifa. Except for specifically non-Jewish sections of the country, the Sabbath is the official day of rest in which all businesses and stores must close."[43]

What is most interesting about Conservative Judaism's allowance for *Shabbat* driving to synagogue[44]—presumably with many people living within fifteen to twenty minutes—is how many people in today's Messianic movement tend to live much further distances from their local congregation. Many people across the Messianic movement know of those who drive an hour or more to attend *Shabbat* services, perhaps from a rural area. While these people may wish to live closer to their congregation's meeting place, or the congregation itself may wish to relocate closer to where many of its people live—economic considerations likely do not permit it.

Beyond the modern Jewish debates of igniting a fire to drive a car, the *JPS Guide to Jewish Traditions* makes a point to note the principle of *pikkuach nefesh*, and specifically how it involves

---

[43] Eisenberg, pp 134-135.

[44] Isaac Klein, *A Guide to Jewish Religious Practice* (New York: The Jewish Theological Seminary of America, 1979), pp 85-86.

feeding the ill, and hence would also likely involve cooking food, as well as making sure that there is a fire for warmth:

"The concept of *pikuach nefesh* is so highly regarded that if a seriously ill person needs food on the Sabbath, the *halakhah* requires that one should slaughter animals and prepare them according to the dietary laws, rather than feed the individual ritually forbidden food. It is even permitted to give patients forbidden food if physicians consider it necessary for their recovery. For three days after giving birth, a woman is considered in a weakened and vulnerable condition. If one of these days falls on a Sabbath, it is an obligation to do everything possible to alleviate her pain and ease her discomfort, including lighting a fire to keep her warm...."[45]

The Exodus 35:3 prohibition on lighting a fire was not given to Ancient Israel, so people could think they could not light a fire in order stay warm during freezing weather. The Exodus 35:3 prohibition, as will be agreed upon by all, was intended to stop fires being lit that would involve or facilitate labor. Today, with our modern conveniences, one can set his or her thermostat to automatically regulate temperatures for both hot and cold, which can limit annoyances for many. The majority of religious Jews do drive on the Sabbath, to their local synagogues, so fellowship among their community is not broken—and in this regard, at least—turning on a car should be thought of as being in a different category than the original Exodus 35:3 instruction. If Conservative Judaism had not made this allowance, than the result could have been an abandonment of *Shabbat* observance altogether, a bigger problem to be sure.

Prohibited Activities for a Modern *Shabbat*

In today's broad Jewish tradition, among Orthodox, Conservative, and even Reform Jews—activities which are believed to be prohibited for the Sabbath, are derived from both Tanach Scripture and ancient tradition, although obviously in different degrees. It can be widely agreed that commerce is prohibited, given how the gates of Jerusalem were shut from merchants on *Shabbat* (Nehemiah 13:15-22). A cessation of work did not apply to guard

[45] Eisenberg, pp 135-136.

duty in the royal court (2 Kings 11:4-12), which by implication would mean that various jobs involved in defense or law enforcement would need to function to some degree on the Sabbath. It also would surely allow for a security detail being present at a synagogue's service, especially with potential acts of anti-Semitism always needing to be spotted. The Shunamite woman would have normally traveled to consult the prophet on the New Moon or Sabbath (2 Kings 4:23), an indication that some form of travel, for religious purposes, would be permitted on *Shabbat*. So, the Conservative Jewish allowance for driving to synagogue on *Shabbat* does have some ancillary Biblical support.

Yeshua the Messiah issued the stern admonition to the lawyers of His day, "Woe to you *Torah* experts too! You load people down with burdens they can hardly bear, and you won't lift a finger to help them!" (Luke 11:46, CJB). The numbers of Rabbinic regulations witnessed in post-Second Temple Jewish literature can certainly seem a bit overbearing for Sabbath observance. Yet, there are useful guidelines to be considered, especially as it concerns the widespread imperative of how whatever can be done before the Sabbath may not be done on the Sabbath. Another principle concerns "Whoever on the Sabbath performs a forbidden act of labor and [the result of] his act of labor endures is liable" (m.*Shabbat* 12:1).[46] *Shabbat* is not supposed to be like the six other days of the week; *Shabbat* is a day of rest and refreshment in God the Creator, and is not a normal day. There are activities that can be conducted at another time, which can wait for *Shabbat* to be concluded.

Jewish scholars, examiners, and thinkers have certainly had to sort through Biblical and extra-Biblical injunctions given for the Sabbath.[47] While there are many examples to be considered, in view of the Tanach prohibition of carrying items on *Shabbat* (cf. Nehemiah 13:15-18)—which various Jews of antiquity took beyond the prohibition of lifting heavy loads[48]—are various Rabbinic injunctions as to what it means to carry an item on *Shabbat*, and

---

[46] Neusner, *Mishnah*, 194.

[47] Cf. the lengthy summation provided by Eisenberg, pp 130-133.

[48] The term employed in Nehemiah 13:19 is *massah* (מַשָּׂא), widely involves "**burden** (of ass, mule...)" or " **burden** = **hardship**" (*CHALOT*, 217).

the boundaries in which an item may or may not be carried. The extra-Biblical term *eruv* (עֵירוּב), technically meaning "*interweaving, mixture, conjunction,*" became associated with "*a symbolical act by which the legal fiction of community* or *continuity is established,*" especially as it regarded "Sabbath limits" (*Jastrow*).[49] The point of establishing an *eruv*, is that carrying an object from one location to another location was prohibited, and so a big common area between homes and families being set up for the Sabbath would circumvent this. The *JPS Guide to Jewish Traditions* summarizes,

> "On the Sabbath, it is forbidden to carry an object (even a house key or handkerchief) outside a private domain, though carrying is permitted inside a private residence or a synagogue. An ingenious way to get around this restriction is to change an object that is usually carried into something that can be worn, such as converting a house key into a tie clip. The prohibition against carrying is especially difficult for mothers of infants or young children. Forbidden to carry a child outside the house, they are effectively confined to their homes on the Sabbath.
>
> "To overcome these restrictions, under certain circumstances the Rabbis permitted the establishment of an *eruv*. Literally meaning 'blending' or 'intermingling,' an *eruv* converts a large public area into a 'private domain' where carrying is permitted on the Sabbath. For example, it is forbidden to carry an object from one house to another. However, if all the tenants living around a large courtyard contribute food and place it at a central point before the Sabbath, the entire area is symbolically transformed from a series of individual private homes into one common group dwelling that belongs to the entire community. Today, a common way of making an *eruv* is to extend a wire or nylon cord around the perimeter of a community, by connecting it to telephone or utility poles. In this way, the entire area becomes a single domain, in which it is permitted to carry and push baby carriages. In Israel, *eruvim* have been constructed in all cities. In the United States, they have been established in cities that have a substantial Orthodox Jewish population."[50]

---

[49] *Jastrow*, 1075.

[50] Eisenberg, pp 133-134.

A strict adherence to the sorts of Sabbath regulations, Biblical and extra-Biblical, summarized above, would be seen in Orthodox Judaism. A consultative approach, recognizing the value that these various traditions had for many Jews of the past, but also evaluating their relevance for the present, is seen in Conservative and Reform Judaism. There are contemporary Conservative Jewish[51] and Reform Jewish discussions on what is permissible for *Shabbat*, with figures from the Conservative[52] and Reform[53] movements both providing modern-day "lists" of what may be constituted as work. While Orthodox traditionalists might be prone to consider Conservative and Reform Jews to be more liberal and permissive than they, it is not as though the latter have totally dismissed both Biblical and extra-Biblical stipulations. In the Reform Jewish publication *Gates of Shabbat*, Mark Dov Shapiro addresses the question, "Why does the Reform approach to Shabbat work and rest differ from that of traditional Judaism?":

> "Reform Jews depart from the traditional definitions of work and rest because we believe that they do not represent the final word on Jewish practice. We maintain that the talmudic sages and their successors only developed definitions of work and rest in response to the specific historic needs of the Jews they knew. The sages themselves even acknowledged that much of their Shabbat legislation was only loosely related to the Torah [referencing m.*Chagigah* 1:8]. Nevertheless, they continued refining their ideas of Shabbat because the biblical Shabbat had to be clarified and elucidated if it was to be followed in their post-biblical world.
>
> "The same holds true for us today. We are 'commanded,' as it were, to continue what Jews have done for centuries. We must develop definitions of work and rest that resonate with the needs of contemporary Jews.
>
> "*One caveat needs to be stated. In creating a contemporary approach to Shabbat, Reform Jews do not function in a vacuum. Although we may depart from ancient*

---

[51] Cf. Isaacs, pp 189-197.

[52] Dresner, pp 80-81.

[53] Shulevitz, pp 95-99; Mark Dov Shapiro, *Gates of Shabbat: A Guide for Observing Shabbat* (New York: Central Conference of American Rabbis, 1996), pp 49-59 provides a summary of what may be considered "rest."

> *practices, we live with a sense of responsibility to the continuum of Jewish experience.*
>
> "Therefore, we try to balance our creativity in practice with the desire to conserve and adapt what speaks to us from the past. We are free to be novel, but proud as well to maintain as much as possible our connections with the best of the Jewish past."[54]

Although there is much that today's Messianic movement would disagree with Reform Judaism about—ranging from its dismissal of the kosher dietary laws,[55] to its non-adherence to the doctrine of the resurrection,[56] to its acceptance of homosexuality—the Reform logic of taking ancient traditions associated with *Shabbat*, and adapting them for more modern times, **is precisely how the Sabbath is observed among many Messianic people.** Today's Messianic people should not feel ashamed if more Center to Leftist branches of Judaism do, in fact, see the intention of the Sabbath instructions as not being hyper-restrictive or set in concrete. While it is important to be aware of the many Orthodox Jewish procedures and applications surrounding *Shabbat*, with most of us noting what they are, recognizing some degree of usefulness for those who observe them, wanting to be sensitive around those who observe them—**we do not feel bound to Sabbath restrictions that go far beyond the intention of Biblical commandments.**

In stark contrast to what is offered in some of the previously quoted summaries, most Messianic people are not going to turn off their smartphones or iPhones on *Shabbat*. They might turn off their phones for their *Shabbat* service on Saturday morning, but there might indeed be legitimate reasons for communicating with fellow Believers using technological devices later on. Most Messianic congregations, in stark contrast to Orthodox Jews who would not even turn on a coffee maker, or add cold milk to coffee or tea—do not consider turning on an electric coffee maker to be work, or

---

[54] Shapiro, 57.

[55] Consult the relevant sections of the *Messianic Kosher Helper* by Messianic Apologetics.

[56] Reform Judaism tends to advocate that the idea of a bodily resurrection was imported into Judaism via Zoroastrian influences in the Persian era.

adding milk to coffee to be baking or boiling. Most Messianic people surely do not consider lathering up with soap, as they shower before going to their congregation—and most assuredly washing their hands—to be a form of "labor." Many Messianic congregations have an *oneg* or refreshment-lunch afterward, which does often require some kind of reheating in an oven.

Making the Effort to Not Work on *Shabbat*

When today's Messianic people seek to be **realistic** about keeping the seventh-day Sabbath or *Shabbat*, while we might recognize the final sacrifice of Yeshua providing atonement for human sin, and astutely recognize that keeping or not keeping the Sabbath is hardly a salvation issue—efforts still need to be taken in order to make the seventh day a holy and blessed time for the people of God. Capital penalties for Sabbath violation might have been absorbed by the Messiah (Colossians 2:14), but loss—both physical and spiritual—is still incurred by people who do not expel the necessary disciplines to make *Shabbat* a time of rest and refreshment. Even many evangelical Christians, albeit with Sunday as the time designated for their day of rest, are recognizing the vast wisdom with a Sabbath-principle—as modern people need to put the ways of the world aside for a day. All too frequently, though, there are people who make excuses for working on the Sabbath, when they have every means at their disposal to legitimately take a rest, and even fellowship with other Believers.

It might be something of a conundrum to say this: **but people need to work in order to set the time aside to rest.** That is, the six days allotted for human beings to work need to be employed as the time for arranging all of the things, that will permit the Sabbath to then be the day set aside for God. This has actually been a huge challenge for many Jewish people in modern America. While we should all be pragmatic enough to recognize that there are times when "life happens," and there are those moments of unavoidable work that will erupt on *Shabbat*—usually in the form of unplanned emergencies—modern people can and will *give in* to the temptation to work on the Sabbath, when reasonable effort can be expelled to postpone things to the business week. Dresner, as a Conservative Jew, addresses the common Jewish dilemma in America, in how many Jews once persecuted and discriminated against in Europe for their Sabbath observance, came to an America that provided religious freedom and opportunity. Alas, though, because of such opportunities to work and build businesses and embrace free enterprise—*Shabbat* has often been a casualty, with too many American Jews dismissing the Sabbath via the guise of their economic interests:

> "Because the Sabbath had the power to preserve the Jew in time of peril, bringing renewal every seven days, the enemies of Israel throughout the ages—in Egypt, Rome, Germany, Russia—have attempted to halt its observance in order to crush the spirit of the people. But everywhere and always the Jewish spirit has triumphed. Everywhere, that is, but America. For America is different! This may very well be the first time in Jewish history when the total Sabbath day, for which Jews willingly made every manner of sacrifice in whatever clime or country they have lived, has been accepted as expendable. See the paradox—what our forefathers were willing to die for when it was forbidden (or at the very least made exceedingly difficult), we dismiss now that we are free to keep it. Only in America, the 'goldene medinah,' was the immigrant Jew too hard put economically to observe the Sabbath.
>
> "If it is true that the Sabbath is the single most important institution of Jewish life and law, if it does indeed contain within itself all of Judaism in miniature, and if it is a fact that without the Sabbath our tradition cannot endure, then how has it been permitted to fall into virtual obsolescence in America? Our continued coexistence with a Sabbath-less Jewry may blur our understanding of how radically new is the situation which confronts us in the American Jewish community. There is little awareness left of the total Sabbath in many congregations. I do not mean an informed keeping of each and every Sabbath law, but at the very least an understanding that Sabbath observance, in the sense of withdrawal from weekday concerns and attachment to the spiritual, as a significant and central goal for American Jews. Few are the congregations, for example, where Sabbath observance or even regular attendance on Sabbath morning is expected of men and women who hold office in that congregation.
>
> "It is claimed that modern times present implacable obstacles before Sabbath observance. Is this really so? Of course, there are problems today that did not exist in the

insulated ghetto of yesterday. But how can one explain the fact that in some communities today the synagogues are very well attended on Sabbath morning and Jews keep the Sabbath, while in other communities the reverse is the case. A study of such communities will disclose that those who keep the Sabbath do not hold jobs different in kind from those who do not. The reason must be sought elsewhere.

"We have made a tragic blunder by excusing Sabbath violation in the name of financial need, a shibboleth that has paralyzed our attempts to apply the Sabbath commandment to the American Jew. An unpleasant fact must be faced: there is simply no correlation—as some believed there was—between greater leisure or financial well-being and Sabbath observance! The reverse is often the case. Though we are no longer poverty-stricken immigrants and leisure time is heavy on our hands, it has made little difference. If Jews wanted to keep the Sabbath, many, if not most, could.

"The Jewish professional determines his own hours and could shift his Wednesday afternoon off to Saturday. The Jewish manufacturer and those associated with manufacturing usually work a five-day week. The Jewish retailer is in a more difficult position. Yet those who close their stores on Sabbath and holidays (and perhaps remain open on Sunday) find the reward well worth the sacrifice. There are others who are dependent upon their employers' terms. Most employees, however, will be surprised at the acceptance with which their Sabbath requests are met. Employers know that a man sincere in his religion usually makes a good worker. Further, special Jewish vocational and employment agencies are available, and fair employment laws forbidding discrimination against Sabbath observers have done much to ease the situation in recent years.

"We are not helpless victims of economic laws. That would be Marxism. Jews have traditionally subjugated the law of man to the law of God which is in truth is the law of man.

"Shall we give up the Sabbath? Shall we do without it for a little more comfort, a little greater affluence?"[57]

While there are surely situations that one will encounter in the course of life, which may require working on the Sabbath from time to time—that unexpected schedule at work, an economic crunch which hits the family requiring a little more work, or an unforeseen

---

[57] Dresner, pp 72-74.

emergency—reasonable sacrifices can be made by many people in order for them to keep *Shabbat*. **Too much really does surround how serious people are about keeping *Shabbat*.** Conservative Jews and Reform Jews have been noted to dismiss the Sabbath, at least in part, or entirely, by placing their economic and business interests at a higher level than making *Shabbat* rest a priority. Orthodox Jews in America, however, have often been able to find ways around some of the challenges. Finkelman observes in his book *Shabbos*, how many Orthodox Jews, at least, took the post-Holocaust and post-World War II period in the West, as a time to turn things around and rebuild lost Torah institutions:

> "...It may well be that, in the aftermath of the Holocaust, God deemed it necessary to shower success and prosperity upon the Jews of the free world, in order to enable them to turn their energies to the creation of a renaissance of Torah life. Are we so much better than our grandparents who failed to withstand the test of assimilation in the West, during years when Sabbath observance meant the weekly loss of a job and the prospect of coming home to crying children and a wife who had nothing to cook for supper?
>
> "Thanks to the relative prosperity of the post-War period and the inspirational leadership of great leaders to whom comfort was meaningless, large numbers of Jews channeled their human and material resources into the task of rebuilding Torah life and institutions throughout the world. So it is that there are outstanding Torah institutions and new armies of Torah adherents in places where, in earlier years, huge Jewish populations had permitted Judaism to decline and whose forbearers were convinced that their Jewish roots were doomed to wither."[58]

There are many, in the Jewish community for certain, who in their wanting to keep *Shabbat* or the festivals, do run into issues with their employers. In his book *Kosher Living*, Isaacs notes the question, "Is it kosher for a person who observes the Sabbath to ask for time off on Jewish holidays without being penalized?" Given some of the economic realities of our time, if refusing to work on *Shabbat* in a particular job, some might be negatively evaluated, or

---

[58] Finkelman, 6.

they might even be terminated. Usually, though, as Isaacs describes, employers will have to recognize the various religious needs of people taking off time for the Sabbath and holidays:

> "It is certainly kosher if one is observant to let his or her employer know at the outset that he or she is an observant Jew and will need to observe a number of Jewish holidays during the year. However, it is not a kosher expectation to think that the employer will acquiesce to giving him or her all these days off with pay or with no obligation to make up the missed work.
>
> "Many observant Jews who choose not to work on the Jewish holidays will often come in to work on a Sunday, work at home, or work late into the night to be sure to finish all that is part of his or her responsibility. This is the fair and kosher thing to do, for when an employer hires a worker, the employer should reasonably expect that the employee will do the job agreed as in the contract."[59]

Saturday is the major day that an employer will need to work with in terms of employees not being able to show up for work. The Jewish community is not the only religious community that observes the seventh-day Sabbath, as various denominations like the Seventh-Day Adventist Church also do keep the Sabbath, and have often been able to help secure special legal dispensations for Sabbatarians. Still, the primary responsibility in making sure that *Shabbat* is set aside as a day of rest and refreshment, as well as fellowship with brethren, is up to individuals and families. You have to consciously place a value on what *Shabbat* is, and make sure that you get the most out of it. Too many have the economic freedom of not having to do any work on Saturday, and they could indeed make the Sabbath a holy time, **but they instead (willfully) forfeit its blessings.**

Messianic Believers Keeping *Shabbat*

The only way that any of us would possibly know who fellow Messianic brothers and sisters are, is by meeting them in person at a Messianic congregation, most probably on Saturday morning. This is true whether these people are Jewish Believers, some of whom

---

[59] Isaacs, pp 82-83.

were raised in a synagogue setting, and later came to faith in Yeshua—or whether they are non-Jewish Believers, led by the Lord to embrace their Hebraic Roots and live a Torah obedient life like the Messiah. Many have a home *Shabbat* dinner with the traditions of candle lighting, *kiddush*, and *challah*—and will frequently open it up to people in their congregations, and/or various other guests. Many, attending worship services on *Shabbat*, may attend congregational classes held a little earlier, or held in the afternoon. Many congregations have a time of fellowship afterward, including refreshments or even a meal. For many Messianic Believers, with their local congregation as the focal point of *Shabbat*, a good part of their day is spent on things of the Lord, with little temptation to break the Sabbath. This is especially true for those assemblies which hold *Havdallah*, and may even have a *chavurah* gathering for Saturday evening (at least on some kind of a semi-regular basis).[60]

Of course, Messianic congregations do vary across the spectrum. Some hold their worship services on *Erev Shabbat* or Friday evening, leaving various individuals and families to develop different routines for the full day following on Saturday. Others will hold services on Saturday morning, but will not set aside a time for fellowship afterward on Saturday afternoon. Other congregations may hold their main services in the afternoon on Saturday, closing it with *Havdallah*.

Even with variance to be expected among Messianic people, one will easily encounter men and women, Jewish and non-Jewish alike, who are quite keen on making *Shabbat* a sanctified time unto the Lord. While congregational service times may vary, and personal and family routines and customs may differ—many are sincere about not working, they want to experience a period of rest and refreshment, and they recognize how fellowshipping on the Sabbath is something quite Biblical. There are those who vary in their Sabbath commitments, among today's Messianic people. Very, very few would be found to keep *Shabbat* at the same level of observance as the Orthodox Synagogue, because most Messianic people will be found driving cars to *Shabbat* services. The bulk of Messianic people desiring to honor *Shabbat* will, however, be found

---

[60] The term *chavurah* (חֲבֵרָא) mainly means "*friend, neighbor, fellow-being*" (*Jastrow*, 422).

to hold to a level of observance consistent somewhere between the Conservative and Reform movements. And, for many—**who need *Shabbat* to be a more conscious reality**—important cues can be taken from how many non-observant Jews, usually Reform, use *Shabbat* as a time to focus on their heritage, and incrementally and steadily begin to evaluate their relationship with God. As Ruth Perelson describes in *Invitation to Shabbat*,

> "Shabbat is a point on which Jews should focus their attention. The observance of Shabbat has been consistently stressed—although in different forms at different times—with a variety of options for observance and celebration. In our freedom to determine what our own Shabbat observance will be, we are not free to ignore Shabbat, for 'How can the Sabbath protect us if we don't protect the Sabbath?'
>
> "We can begin by learning about Shabbat and raising our consciousness of it. We can yet move on to increments of observance, a little at a time, as we become more knowledgeable and comfortable with them. From consciousness-raising, we can move on to such positive acts as lighting candles, having a festive meal, attending synagogue, planning Shabbat events that we feel—as individuals or as families—are in keeping with Shabbat, and making *Havdalah*.
>
> "In other words, when I say Shabbat, I refer to its totality as a concept, and I ask you to consider it in that way for yourselves. Some of what we do on Shabbat we do as individuals; some we undertake as part of a family, congregation, or other group. All our Shabbat observances are, of course, highly personal. This is a legitimate and historic Jewish approach, although many Jews do not think about Shabbat in terms of all of these dimensions.
>
> "If you have come this far with me, let me ask you some questions that I ask myself: Are we prepared to talk about Shabbat making demands on us? Are we as individuals prepared to educate ourselves so that we can make informed choices about the observance of Shabbat? Our answers to these questions may lead to changes in the way we live our lives, in the manner in which our synagogues function, and, indeed, in how we define being a Jew."[61]

---

[61] Ruth Perelson, *An Invitation to Shabbat: A Beginner's Guide to Weekly Celebration* (New York: UAHC Press, 1997), 54.

Of course, various Jewish people, trying to rediscover their heritage, will inevitably find out that not all of their questions of human existence are answered, and so in begging God to reveal Himself, **may discover that Yeshua is the Messiah of Israel!** Non-Jewish Believers, however, knowing that Yeshua is the Savior, tend to want to be more like Him, and today are being drawn toward the Sabbath. In so doing, many of the patterns of incrementally investigating the significance of *Shabbat*, steadily employing various traditions and customs, and implementing disciplines so that the Sabbath can be a time of rest and refreshment—can be approached in a manner similar to Jews rediscovering their heritage.

Individuals and families, in their quest to honor the Sabbath—obviously outside of congregational activities—will have to wrestle, or at least reason, with Biblical directions and traditional approaches, about what it means to make *Shabbat* a holy time. **This is where many of us need to give one another a wide berth,** not only for recognizing those areas where exceptions for work and life situations present themselves, but also for being responsible for our own Sabbath observance *first*, before intruding into the lives of others. The most that any rabbi or spiritual leader can often do, is provide a list of personal observances, offering suggestions to others. Isaacs answers the question "What kosher activities can I do on Shabbat afternoon?" with a list of activities that he likely does, as a Conservative rabbi:

"Taking a walk, napping, playing a board game, reading for pleasure, and studying Torah are all appropriate activities for the afternoon of the Sabbath. In the summer months beginning with the Sabbath after Passover, the custom is to read and study Pirkei Avot (Ethics of the Fathers), a Talmudic tractate that teaches one how to be a better person."[62]

Indeed, many people will return home from congregational services mid-afternoon, and take a nap. They will then be awake as the Sabbath closes, avoiding any major opportunity to violate *Shabbat* via unnecessary work. Others return home, and rest in other ways.

---

[62] Isaacs, 192.

The biggest, and most preventable temptation that exists in many Messianic congregations, which can violate the *Shabbat* restriction of engaging in unnecessary commerce, is how many, when their *Shabbat* morning service is over, will go out to eat at a restaurant for lunch. While Messianic Jewish Believers, particularly in North America, are not immune from this—this is actually more of an import to the Messianic movement from non-Jewish Believers who went out to lunch after Sunday church services. Some of the reasons for going out to lunch, after *Shabbat* morning services, might be to fellowship with fellow Messianic Believers, who are not seen during the normal week and may have to travel some distance to a congregation. Yet, many Messianic congregations can and do offer refreshments or a lunch after morning services, not only to prevent unnecessary commerce, like going to a restaurant for lunch, but to encourage community interaction. Of course, various people in a congregation or fellowship might still leave when the service is over, and go to lunch with a number of their congregants. Mechanisms can and should be in place to discourage this.[63]

Being Realistic About *Shabbat*

The weekly Sabbath or *Shabbat* presents a great opportunity to those who make the effort to welcome it, abstain from their labors, and enter into the rest of God. The Sabbath especially tends to be an anticipated feature of Messianic Believers who live in the United States, because unlike any other Western country, the U.S. has no mandated vacations, quite contrary to Europe.[64] Many people do not get to take extensive holidays, **and so a weekly respite on *Shabbat* should be something embraced!** This will require all of us to expel efforts throughout the working week to make sure that *Shabbat* is set aside, requiring each of us to pre-plan many things.

The vast majority of Messianic people are not going to keep *Shabbat* as those in Orthodox Judaism. Some might consider their level of Sabbath observance to be "Conservadox," more like Conservative Judaism but leaning toward Orthodox. In on the

---

[63] Issues pertaining to the kosher keeping of Messianic people, and eating out at restaurants, is worthy of examination for sure. Consult the FAQ, "Public Restaurants, Kosher," and for a wider discussion, the *Messianic Kosher Helper* by Messianic Apologetics.

[64] Shulevitz, pp 207-208.

ground circumstances, the bulk of those striving to make *Shabbat* a holy time, are going to end up with a style that is actually "Reformative," more like Reform Judaism but leaning Conservative. **What this notably does not include are people who treat *Shabbat* as a kind of "Saturday church,"** as though it is exclusively about attending a worship service with fellow Believers, and the requirement to rest does not extend into one's home and toward one's person.

While uniformity regarding Messianic Sabbath observance should be no more expected than the uniformity which is lacking among different branches of the Jewish Synagogue, more effort does need to be employed by each of us in reasoning through activities which are permitted and prohibited, as well as classifying those legitimate "emergency" situations which require commercial transactions and labor. **Different levels of Sabbath observance will be present among individuals who compose congregations and fellowships.** While each individual is ultimately responsible before the Lord, an environment that encourages obedience, and leads via a Sabbath rest tempered with the love and mercy of the Messiah, is what needs to be facilitated. People who are keeping the Sabbath properly, and are being refreshed in Him, should be demonstrating His salvation in a way so that others will want to join in!

Interestingly enough, what may very well emerge among those serious about *Shabbat*, is that the conduct of many Messianic people might not be too different than that of many pietistic Christian people who kept the "Sunday Sabbath" of yesteryear. These people would have recognized the day of rest as a time to focus on God, one's fellow Believers, and would have avoided those activities of pure pleasure, when human beings—and not human beings *and* their Creator—would have been the focus.

About the Author

John Kimball McKee is an integral part of Outreach Israel Ministries, and serves as the editor of Messianic Apologetics. He is a graduate of the University of Oklahoma (Class of 2003) with a B.A. in political science, and holds an M.A. in Biblical Studies from Asbury Theological Seminary (Class of 2009). He is a 2009 recipient of the Zondervan Biblical Languages Award for Greek. John has held memberships in the Evangelical Theological Society, the Evangelical Philosophical Society, and Christians for Biblical Equality, and is a longtime supporter of the perspectives and views of the Creationist ministry of Reasons to Believe. In 2019, John was licensed as a Messianic Teacher with the International Alliance of Messianic Congregations and Synagogues (IAMCS).

Since the 1990s, John's ministry has capitalized on the Internet's ability to reach people all over this planet. He has spoken with challenging and probing articles to a wide Messianic audience, and those evangelical Believers who are interested in Messianic things. Given his generational family background in evangelical ministry, as well as in academics and the military, John carries a strong burden to assist in the development and maturation of our emerging Messianic theology and spirituality. John has had the profound opportunity since 1997 to engage many in dialogue, so that they will consider the questions he postulates, as his only agenda is to be as Scripturally sound as possible. John believes in demonstrating a great deal of honor and respect to both his evangelical Protestant, Wesleyan and Reformed family background, as well as to the Jewish Synagogue, and together allowing the strengths and virtues of our Judeo-Protestant heritage to be employed for the Lord's plan for the Messianic movement in the long term future.

J.K. McKee is the son of the late K. Kimball McKee (1951-1992) and Margaret Jeffries McKee Huey (1953-), and stepson of William Mark Huey (1951-), who married his mother in 1994, and who is the executive director of Outreach Israel Ministries. Mark Huey is the Director of Partner Relations for the Joseph Project, a ministry of the Messianic Jewish Alliance of America (MJAA).

John has a very strong appreciation for those who have preceded him. His father, Kimball McKee, was a licensed lay minister in the Kentucky Conference of the United Methodist Church, and was a very strong evangelical Believer, most appreciable of the Jewish Roots of the faith. Among his many ministry pursuits, Kim brought the Passover *seder* to

Christ United Methodist Church in Florence, KY, was a Sunday school teacher, and was extremely active in the Walk to Emmaus, leading the first men's walk in Madras, India in 1991. John is the grandson of the late Prof. William W. Jeffries (1914-1989; CDR USN WWII), who served as a professor at the United States Naval Academy in Annapolis, MD from 1942-1989, notably as the museum director and founder of what is now the William W. Jeffries Memorial Archives in the Nimitz Library. John is the great-grandson of Bishop Marvin A. Franklin (1894-1972), who served as a minister and bishop of the Methodist Church, throughout his ministry serving churches in Georgia, Florida, Alabama, and Mississippi. Bishop Franklin was President of the Council of Bishops from 1959-1960. John is also the first cousin twice removed of the late Charles L. Allen (1913-2005), formerly the senior pastor of Grace Methodist Church of Atlanta, GA and First Methodist Church of Houston, TX, and author of numerous books, notably including *God's Psychiatry*. John can also count among his ancestors, Lt. Colonel, By Brevet, Dr. James Cooper McKee (1830-1897), a Union veteran of the U.S. Civil War and significant contributor to the medical science of his generation.

J.K. McKee is a native of the Northern Kentucky/Greater Cincinnati, OH area. He has also lived in Dallas, TX, Norman, OK, Kissimmee-St. Cloud, FL, and Roatán, Honduras, Central America. He presently resides in McKinney, TX, just north of Dallas.

After reading the primer *Shabbat: Sabbath for Messianic Believers*, you should be interested in the much larger, *Messianic Sabbath Helper*

The instruction to remember the Sabbath is the Fourth of the Ten Commandments: "Remember the sabbath day, to keep it holy. Six days you shall labor and do all your work, but the seventh day is a sabbath of the LORD your God; *in it* you shall not do any work" (Exodus 20:8-10a). The seventh-day Sabbath or *Shabbat* is widely associated with God's creation of the world (Genesis 2:2-3) and the Exodus of Ancient Israel from Egypt (Deuteronomy 15:15). The Sabbath is one of the Torah's *moedim* or appointed times (Leviticus 23:3). Desecration of the Sabbath actually brought judgment to Ancient Israel (Jeremiah 17:19-27), but blessings are offered to those who value and honor *Shabbat* (Isaiah 56:1-8), with a universal observance for the entire world anticipated in the Messianic Age (Isaiah 66:23).

Today's Messianic movement is different from evangelical Christianity, in that while it affirms the Messiahship of Yeshua (Jesus) of Nazareth, it continues to observe the seventh-day Sabbath along with Judaism, in fidelity to the Torah or Law of Moses, and in conjunction with the example of the First Century Believers. Certainly, holding services on the seventh-day (commonly called Saturday), can be viewed as appropriate for a faith community identifying with the Jewish Synagogue, but it also raises many questions. *Inquiries abound pertaining to the ongoing validity of the Sabbath in the post-resurrection era.* Was not the Sabbath transferred to Sunday, in honor of the Messiah's being raised from the dead? Was the Sabbath actually abolished by the Messiah? *Inquiries abound pertaining to the observance of the Sabbath.* Should not the Sabbath be kept according to the Scriptures only? Should not mainstream Jewish tradition and custom play some role in honoring the Sabbath? What does it mean to not "work" on *Shabbat?*

The *Messianic Sabbath Helper* includes a wide breadth of material, addressing a wide array of topics associated with *Shabbat*. This publication has been divided up into two main parts: *The Significance of Shabbat* and *A Theology of Shabbat*. You will be able to detect a progression of sorts, in our family's own approach to the subject matter, as some things are addressed first more generally and then more specifically. In our experience, we ourselves have certainly had to move from a more elementary view of the issue of the seventh-day Sabbath, to a more developed view, and we recognize how the Messianic community needs to do the same.

This is a massive collection of material, well needed for every Messianic home and congregational library!

the following list of Bible passages are dealt with extensively in the Messianic Sabbath Helper

Genesis 2:1-3
Exodus 16:22-30
Exodus 20:8-11
Exodus 23:12; 34:21
Exodus 31:12-17
Exodus 35:1-3
Leviticus 19:3, 30; 26:2
Leviticus 23:1-3
Leviticus 24:5-9
Numbers 15:32-36
Numbers 28:9-10
Deuteronomy 5:12-15
Isaiah 1:13-14
Isaiah 56:1-8
Isaiah 58:13-14
Isaiah 66:23
Jeremiah 17:19-27
Ezekiel 20:23-31
Ezekiel 22:8-26
Ezekiel 23:38
Ezekiel 44:24
Ezekiel 45:17
Ezekiel 46:1-4, 12
Hosea 2:11
Amos 8:4-6
Psalm 92:1-2
Nehemiah 9:14
Nehemiah 10:31-34
Nehemiah 13:15-22
Matthew 5:17-19
Mark 1:21-22; Luke 4:16
Mark 2:23-28; Matthew 12:1-8; Luke 6:1-5
Mark 3:1-6; Matthew 12:9-14; Luke 6:6-11
Mark 6:1-2
Matthew 24:20
Mark 16:1; Matthew 28:1; Luke 24:1
Luke 13:10-17
Luke 14:1-6
John 5:1-18
John 7:21-24
John 9:1-16
Acts 1:12
Acts 13:14, 42-44
Acts 15:19-21
Acts 16:13; 17:2
Acts 18:1-8
Acts 20:7
Romans 14
1 Corinthians 16:1-2
Galatians 4:8-11
Colossians 2:16-23
Hebrews 4:1-10
Revelation 1:10

Passover per Parable of the Vineyard

02/19/2021 Unleavened bread

— Remember Forever —

Read Ex 12 + 13 EGYPT

Yahuah's Paseach —

Girded loins w/ shoes on!

1st DAY
7th DAY > Holy Assembly

Feast Unleavened Bread forever

Eve 14

WHY DO we celebrate Feasts, HD

Memorial to Yahuah Forever —

Deut 16:5-6 — Today Forever Only Jerusalem

To ones in the Promise Land
We are now in EGYPT
MOST HIGH DWELLS — (ACTS 7:48-50 — MT 18:20)

Yeast BS BP Breads tart Crole

KOSHER Lamb

4/27 // 428 — May 4

Made in the USA
Coppell, TX
31 December 2020

Flesh Matza Herbs

Burn excess — Ex 12 8-11

47369832R00095

Halal